A Sunlit Absence

A Sunlit Absence

Silence, Awareness,
and Contemplation

Martin Laird, O.S.A.

OXFORD
UNIVERSITY PRESS

Oxford University Press, Inc., publishes works that further
Oxford University's objective of excellence
in research, scholarship, and education.

Oxford   New York

Auckland   Cape Town   Dar es Salaam   Hong Kong   Karachi
Kuala Lumpur   Madrid   Melbourne   Mexico City   Nairobi
New Delhi   Shanghai   Taipei   Toronto

With offices in

Argentina   Austria   Brazil   Chile   Czech Republic   France   Greece
Guatemala   Hungary   Italy   Japan   Poland   Portugal   Singapore
South Korea   Switzerland   Thailand   Turkey   Ukraine   Vietnam

Copyright © 2011 by Martin Laird, O.S.A.

Published by Oxford University Press, Inc.
198 Madison Avenue, New York, New York 10016
www.oup.com

Oxford is a registered trademark of Oxford University Press

Library of Congress Cataloging-in-Publication Data
Laird, M. S. (Martin S.)
A sunlit absence : silence, awareness, and contemplation / by Martin Laird.
p. cm.
Includes bibliographical references.
ISBN 978-0-19-537872-6
1. Contemplation.   2. Silence—Religious aspects—Christianity.   I. Title.
BV5091.C7L36 2011
248.3'4—dc22   2010041215

Printed in the United States of America
on acid-free paper

For Monica and Tom Cornell
of The Catholic Worker

I am.
  —Exodus 3:14

Remain in me.
  —John 15:4

You were within me, Lord, but I was outside myself.
  —Saint Augustine

You are the space that embraces my being and buries it in yourself.
  —Edith Stein

Here's the thing, say Shug. The thing I believe. God is inside you and inside everybody else. You come into the world with God. But only them that search for it inside find it.
  —Alice Walker, *The Color Purple*

Contents

Acknowledgments

In contrast to financial debts, those of gratitude bear one up rather than wear one down. My debts of long-standing gratitude are many: to Joan Rieck, who for over twenty years has taught me more about the way of silence than the hush of any forest; to Dom Cyril of St. Hugh's Charterhouse, Parkminster, UK, as well as to Dom Bernard (RIP) of Gaudalupe Abbey, Lafayette, Oregon; to Pauline Matarasso for her steadfast friendship and proofreading skills; Carolyn Osiek, R.S.C.J., to my confreres Paul Graham, O.S.A. and Mark Minihane, O.S.A., at St. Monica's Priory, London, for their generous sharing of early morning silence and for giving me the top floor of the priory in which to work on this book. I remain ever grateful to Werner Valentin for his attentive help in times past, and lastly, to an old friend whom I shall always love.

Cynthia Read at Oxford University Press and Elizabeth Wales at Wales Literary Agency have provided steadying and humane encouragement during difficult periods. Thanks, too, to Lisbeth Redfield for all her technical assistance.

Villanova University has been my academic community and home for the last thirteen years, and I remain grateful for the support of the Department of Theology and Religious Studies. I am especially thankful for the friendship of Christopher Daly, Kevin Hughes, and Thomas Smith, among many other colleagues and friends.

Books are largely written in solitude, and like all fruitful solitude, it is essentially ecclesial, the gift of community. For this my gratitude extends to many. John FitzGerald, O.S.A., Mary Grace Kuppe, O.S.A., Richard Jacobs, O.S.A., Brian Lowery, O.S.A., Thomas Martin, O.S.A., Gerald Nicholas, O.S.A., Benignus O'Rourke, O.S.A., Raymond Ryan, O.S.A., Theodore Tack, O.S.A., James Thompson, O.S.A. I should also like to express my gratitude for the friendship and support of Kay Buxton, Michael Coll, Betty Maney, and Polly Robin. Last but by no means least, the many Carmelite monasteries throughout Great Britain who have welcomed me as their loving brother.

Biblical citations, if not from memory, are from various English translations: the New Jerusalem Bible, the New American Bible, the New Revised Standard Version. Grateful acknowledgment is given for permission to quote the following: Bloodaxe Books, Ltd., for permission to quote from David Scott, *Piecing Together* and R. S. Thomas, *Collected Later Poems*. Pauline Matarasso for permission to quote from *The Price of Admission* (Cambridge, UK: Broughton House Books, 2005). The Orion Publishing Group for permission to quote from R. S. Thomas, *Collected Poems* 1945–1990 (J. M. Dent, an imprint of The Orion Publishing Group, 1993). "Thirteen Ways of Looking at a Blackbird" from *The Collected Poems of Wallace Stevens* by Wallace Stevens, copyright 1954 by Wallace Stevens and renewed 1982 by Holly Stevens, used by permission of Alfred A. Knopf, a division of Random House, Inc., and of Faber and Faber, Inc. The Estate of Robert Penn Warren for permission to quote from "The Enclave," *Selected Poems:* 1923–1975, Random House, Inc., 1975; copyright 1975 by Robert Penn Warren. Excerpt from "Sunlight" from "Mossbawn: Two Poems in Dedication" from *Opened Ground: Selected Poems* 1966–1996 by Seamus Heaney, copyright © 1998 by Seamus Heaney. Reprinted by permission of Farrar, Straus and Giroux, LLC, and of Faber and Faber, Inc.

A Sunlit Absence

Introduction

Hedgehogs and Foxes

Isaiah Berlin and St. Teresa of Avila do not often show up in the same sentence. The twentieth-century British philosopher's most popular essay, *The Hedgehog and the Fox*, famously invokes the ancient Greek poet Archilochus: "the fox knows many things, but the hedgehog knows one big thing."[1] The sixteenth-century Spanish doctor of the Church, St. Teresa of Avila, makes a good case for being a hedgehog, especially in her best-known work, *The Interior Castle*. She knows "one big thing" and this she revisits time and again from different angles throughout her writings: with respect to the relationship between God and the innermost depths of the human person, "it is all about love melting in love."[2] The union between Creator and creature is so utterly convincing that Teresa says it "is like rain falling from the sky into a river or pool. There is nothing but water. It's impossible to divide the sky-water from the land-water."[3] Rainwater is not land-water, but this distinction, though real, is practically speaking at a remove from the experience itself. "When a little stream enters the sea, who could separate its waters back out again?"[4] Freshwater is not saltwater, but the two cannot be separated in the bay of our creation in the image and likeness of God (Gn 1:26). Furthermore St. Teresa bids us to liken this union between God and the human person to "a bright light pouring into a room from two large windows: it enters from different places but becomes one light."[5] Teresa is trying to express in words the central paradox that lies at the heart of the relationship between Creator and creature, the paradox of union-in-difference.

This book, like its companion volume, *Into the Silent Land*, is also about "one big thing."[6] By the grace of creation and redemption, there is a grounding union between God and the human person. In the depths of this ground, the "between" cannot be perceived, for it is completely porous to the Divine Presence. Indeed there is more Presence than preposition. While this is the simplest and most fundamental fact of our spiritual lives, it takes a lifetime to realize it. Though this grounding union "in which we live and move and have our being" (Acts 17–28) is unshakable, one of the characteristics of the human condition is that we spend many decades of our lives in sheer ignorance of this. The reason for our ignorance of the most obvious and simplest of facts about our spiritual life is the constant inner noise and chatter that creates and sustains the illusion of being separate from God, who, as St. Augustine reminds us, is already, "closer to me than I am to myself."[7]

If inner noise sustains this perceived alienation from our inmost selves, we shall feel perforce alienated from God. But this sense of alienation or separation is generated by blind and noisy ignorance that insinuates itself in the surface regions of our awareness. Our culture for the most part trains us to keep our attention riveted to this surface noise, which in turn maintains the illusion of God as a distant object for which we must seek as for something we are convinced we lack. One of the great mysteries of the contemplative path is the discovery that, when the veils of separation drop, we see that the God we have been seeking has already found us, knows us, and sustains us in being from all eternity. Indeed, "God is your being," as the author of the *Cloud of Unknowing* says (though we are not God's being).[8]

We should not underestimate just how persuasive the noise in our heads can be. Saint Augustine's friend, Alypius, provides a vivid portrayal of this when St. Augustine describes Alypius's nearly addictive relationship to the entertainment industry of the day, Rome's gladiatorial games. Saint Augustine tells us that Alypius "had been seized by an incredible obsession for gladiatorial spectacles and to an unbelievable degree."[9] He did his best to hold these "spectacles in aversion and detestation." But one evening some friends used "friendly violence" to take him to the games.[10] He was determined to keep his eyes closed throughout the spectacle. But no sooner did he hear the crowd roar as a man fell in combat than he opened his eyes and "was struck in the soul by a wound graver than the gladiator in his body, whose fall caused the roar. The shouting entered by his ears and forced open his eyes."[11] Alypius was helpless. "His eyes were riveted. He imbibed madness. Without any awareness of what was happening to him, he found delight in the murderous contest and was inebriated by bloodthirsty pleasure. He was not now the person who came in."[12]

Saint Augustine astutely observes the ordeal that befell his friend and future saint. Alypius was "without any awareness of what was happening to him." As a result "he was not now the same person" once he set eyes on the gladiatorial games. Awareness is somehow the key to who we are.

Spiritual traditions devote a good deal of attention to the ever-changing landscape that is awareness. Our awareness has its flat, rugged prairies, but also its mountains and precipices. As Gerard Manley Hopkins puts it:

O the mind, mind has mountains; cliffs of fall
Frightful, sheer, no-man-fathomed.[13]

These depths must be explored; for they bottom out in God, the depthless depth that is the ground of all.

This book is concerned to show how the Christian tradition of the practice of contemplation is as much concerned with the expansion of awareness as it is with the concentration of our attention on a prayer word or phrase. In fact expansion of awareness and the concentration of attention are two sides of the coin of our spirit. They are as one.

This book will unfold in the following manner. For those who did not read the companion volume *Into the Silent Land*, chapter 1 will present key aspects of that book's central concern, which carries over into this book, namely our experience of distractions. Distractions are a given in the practice of contemplation; our practice cannot deepen without them. What changes over the course of time is our relationship with them. Gradually we see that distractions contain within themselves the silence we seek; therefore, we do not have to be rid of them in order for our practice of contemplation to open up.

In chapter 2 we shall see the world of distraction in full force by listening to how university students draw on the wisdom of the fourth-century monk Evagrius to gain insight into their own problems. As a result we, too, gain insight

into some of the struggles we each must face if we are to discover stillness within.

Silence plays a crucial role in the spiritual life. Environmental silence is the soil in which a healthy contemplative
practice takes root. But can silence be reduced to the absence of
sound waves? Chapter 3 explores some fundamental truths
about silence: it has no opposite and is the ground of both sound
and the absence of sound. Moreover, silence is intrinsically
related to the expansion of our own awareness. The deepening
of concentration through the use of a prayer word or prayer
phrase is of a piece with the expansion of awareness.

Expansion of awareness does not mean that we become
aware of yet more things. This book concerns the expansion
that takes place *within* awareness itself, before awareness
becomes awareness *of* this or that object. It is the blossoming
within awareness (from the inside out as it were) of the flowing luminous vastness that is interior silence. This silent,
flowing awareness is untouched by noise and turmoil and yet
at the same time is generous and open enough to ground
both calm and calamity. Chapter 4 shows how the Christian
contemplative tradition sees this expansion of luminous
awareness in the framework of a threefold dynamic.

As growth takes place, pain occurs. This is true of life gen-
erally and abundantly so of the life of prayer. Prayer deepens
by way of ordeal. Chapters 5, 6, and 7 explore some of the
facets of these ordeals that emerge as a result of the gradual

blossoming of awareness. It hurts for a bud to bloom. In this process, as chapter 5 will show, boredom plays a pivotal role as we begin to discover a silence that is deeper than what the surface faculties of the mind can perceive. In an entertainment culture such as ours, this onset of boredom in prayer can come as a rather rude awakening. While we may feel we are losing our prayer life, it is actually deepening. Chapter 6 considers how the practice of contemplation can help loosen the grip of depression and panic in our lives. Chapter 7 frames a view onto an even deeper pain. It is one thing to learn to accept a certain boredom that accompanies spiritual growth; it is quite another to become acutely aware of one's own arrogance, judgmentalism, envy, or overconcern for reputation (vainglory). When we have long grown accustomed to the sands of boredom in prayer and begin to become aware of these intellectual sins, we are immersed in what St. John of the Cross calls "sharp trials in the intellect." These trials are neither for the beginner nor for the impatient.

Chapter 8 is a freestanding chapter that assembles responses to some of the more common questions and concerns people have made known to me through e-mail or during public lectures.

Throughout this book there has been a deliberate decision to remain within the Christian tradition. While Buddhism, Hinduism, and many other spiritual traditions have very much indeed that is wise and useful to say about concentration and awareness, Christian wisdom on the subject is little known among Christians themselves. Many Christians are surprised to learn that Christianity has anything at all to say on these matters.

Not only does this book include abundant examples drawn from among the writings of ancient Christian saints and sages—as well as from modern authors (chiefly poets)—to highlight a point or to advance a thesis, but there are also stories and struggles of present-day spiritual pilgrims. Normal people. For those of us who walk the path of contemplation, it is important to see that, while our individual stories are unique and personal, they are shared by us all. It is a relief to see that our own pain, struggle, loss, joy, and victory are woven into the much larger fabric of all those who seek the face of God (Ps 27:8).

Evagrius says, "Be like an astute business man: make stillness be your criterion for testing the value of everything, and choose always what contributes to it."[14] As we struggle to sit still in prayer today or any day, we become part of a living tradition that stretches back centuries, witnessing to the fact that the God we seek has already sought and found us from all eternity: "Before I formed you in the womb, I knew you" (Jer 1:5).

ONE

Standing at the Gate of the Heart

On the Practice of Contemplation

Stand diligently at the gate of the heart.
  —St. Philotheos

The practice of stillness is full of joy and beauty.
  —Evagrius

THE GATE OF THE HEART

Contemplation is the soul's Copernican revolution. Copernicus did not invent a heliocentric universe. He simply discovered what had always been the case. The sun never did revolve around the earth. The revolution was the integrating glimpse of the truth of things that marked a change in how we see the world. To realize that we do not search for God the way we search for fame, fortune, and fulfillment—or for anything else that we are convinced we lack—is the "pearl of great price" (Mt 13:45–46), the realization that "the Kingdom of God is within you" (Lk 17:21). It signals the beginning of this spiritual revolution.

Saint John of the Cross stated it as simply as he could: "The soul's center is God."[1] Indeed God does not revolve around us any more than the sun revolves around us, despite the evidence of the "I." This Center, however, is not an object like other centers in the middle of something else, like jam or custard in the center of a doughnut. As St. Bonaventure reminds us, "God is an intelligible sphere whose center is everywhere and whose circumference is nowhere."[2] To glimpse this, however fleetingly, is to realize that we are and always have been immersed in unfathomable Vastness that is at the same time as familiar and unremarkable as a bar of soap. This is our home.

The Center reveals itself to be everywhere. "It is within all things," St. Bonaventure continues, "but not enclosed; outside all things, but not excluded."[3] The Center encompasses all things, even as it indwells all things, the way the sea fills the membrane of the sponge that makes its home in the sea. The sponge is itself immersed in the Vastness that indwells it. Yet God's indwelling saturates us even more pervasively. As Angelus Silesius says in his *Cherubinic Wanderer*,

> "God far more dwells in me than if the entire sea,
> Would in a tiny sponge wholly contained be."[4]

The sponge does not seek this out. This is its life. Nor do we seek this out. This is our life. "He is the ocean deep, contained I am in him."[5]

The practice of contemplation is one of the great spiritual arts. Not a technique but a skill, it harnesses the winds of grace that lead us out into the liberating sea of Silence. To navigate this ancient way of prayer is to put out into the deep and let down our nets for a catch (Lk 5:4). Paradoxically we discover that it is we ourselves who are caught and held in this net, an ocean-depth of moment. We realize to our great delight that the knotted netting of our anguished sense of separation from God is already immersed in these waters, where we are cleansed and freshened by its salt (Ez 16:4; 2 Kgs 2:19–21), indeed "seasoned with salt," as St. Augustine puts it.[6]

An earlier book, *Into the Silent Land,* presented this voyage through a biblical metaphor of passing through doorways. "Knock and the door will be opened" (Mt 7:7; Lk 11:9); "Look, I am standing at the door knocking" (Rev 3:2); "I am the door" (Jn 19:9). The key to unlocking these doorways of prayer is our own silence. This inner silence ultimately reveals that we do not have to move through any doors, for Christ is also the door itself. Therefore, at each and every step of the way our fixed notions of progress in the spiritual life fall down in reverent irrelevance before Christ's liberating manifestation: "I am the door" (Jn 19:9).

This chapter serves as a hinge between *Into the Silent Land* and this companion volume, joining the key insights and dynamics of the practice of contemplation to the themes that will be addressed in the chapters that follow. The key insight is this: as our practice matures and deepens, so will our experience of the ordeals, sorrows, and joys of life, however they happen to be at any given moment, also expand into generous, receptive maturity.

The more we practice, the more our practice develops. It is something like baking bread. Before the dough even gets into the oven, the baker turns the dough out on the table for kneading. At first the dough is stiff and awkward, but after kneading, it becomes responsive and lighter. After being kneaded, left to rest and rise, the dough takes on new texture before being placed in the oven. What finally emerges is very different from what went in. And so with the practice of contemplation. At first our practice seems stiff and awkward, but after sufficient time and dedication it takes on a different character.

CHRISTIAN ROOTS OF THE PRACTICE OF CONTEMPLATION

For Christians Jesus himself is the prime example of the practice of contemplation. According to early Christian contemplatives, this example is not the healing of the demoniac, the rebuking of the winds, or the Transfiguration, but Jesus' own temptation in the desert (Mt 4:1–11). The ordeal in prayer is fundamentally a battle with thoughts, and the early contemplatives noticed something vitally important in how

Jesus dealt with the thoughts by which Satan tried to ensnare him. The fourth-century monk Evagrius spoke for generations of early Christian contemplatives when he observed that Jesus "passed on to us what he did when tempted by Satan. In the moment of struggle, when the demons attack us with pricks and darts, we must answer them with a verse from Holy Scripture."[7] Listening attentively to the account of Jesus' temptation in the desert, Evagrius and others like him observed that Jesus avoided getting caught up in any sort of conversation with Satan. Instead, Jesus quoted lines of Scripture (from Deuteronomy), in order to break the cycle of inner chatter that would only hold his attention captive the more he listened to it and indulged it.

Jesus' own battle with thoughts becomes, then, the Christian foundation of the practice of contemplation: the quiet repetition of a scriptural phrase in order to keep the attention focused. This became a common practice among the desert fathers and mothers who memorized passages of Scripture (sometimes lengthy passages) in order to break free of this snare of thoughts.[8] Saint Augustine referred to these as "arrow prayers."[9] Scripture also claims, however, that the name of Jesus itself casts out demons (Lk 10:17) and implies the presence of the Holy Spirit (1 Cor 12:3). Thus the quiet repetition of "Jesus" as an anchor in the midst of a storm, what today we might call a prayer word, has come to be known as the Jesus Prayer.

Down through the centuries, the Jesus Prayer has taken various forms, from a single word, "Jesus," to the lengthier "Jesus Christ, Son of [the living] God, have mercy on me [a sinner]."[10] Saint John Climacus provides some of the most succinct instruction of all, "Let the remembrance of Jesus be with your every breath. Then indeed you will appreciate the value of stillness."[11]

The practice of contemplation in the Christian tradition tends to emphasize the cultivation of concentration through the use of a short phrase or prayer word (*versiculum*), often inspired by Scripture. But this is not the only way to dispose ourselves to the gift of contemplation. The Carthusian monk Guigo II explains in his *Ladder of Monks* something he inherited as a way of reading and resting in Scripture in such a way that we are ultimately drawn into repose in the silence of Scripture.[12] This is known as *lectio divina* and is a style of prayer with deep roots in the Christian tradition. Saint John of the Cross does not appear to focus on the use of a prayer word to concentrate the mind, but instead on the cultivation of awareness: "Preserve a loving attentiveness to God with no desire to feel or understand any particular thing concerning him."[13] These general approaches to the practice of contemplation, however, are not opposed to each other; for the interior silence that all contemplative practices cultivate finally blossoms as luminous, flowing awareness, not awareness of objects that come and go in the mind like changing weather, but the simple opening up from within of the ground of awareness, before it becomes awareness of this or that object. For many, prayer will simply become (whether or not the prayer word is used) just being; simple sitting in awareness. This is a luminous and solid seat. But most find, at least early on, the use of some sort of anchor like the prayer word to be a great support in reining in the wandering roving mind.

"KNOCK AND THE DOOR SHALL BE OPENED" (MT 7:7; LK 11:9)

"Let us sit still and keep our attention fixed within ourselves," says Evagrius.[14] Simone Weil describes prayer in much the same spirit when she says "Prayer consists of attention," and "the quality of the attention counts for much in the quality of the prayer."[15] The practice of contemplation begins with our attention and our bodies.

The basics are simple. We sit down and assume a solid, erect posture. Saint. Gregory of Sinai recommends sitting on "a seat about nine inches high."[16] Nowadays we call this a prayer bench, which we place over our calves and sit on, with the back straight but not rigid. The bench is angled to facilitate the back's natural s-curve and encourages a sturdy, alert posture. These prayer benches are fairly popular, quite googleable, and not especially inexpensive. Still others prefer a prayer cushion. But most prefer to sit in a chair. In any case the body's solid, stable posture contributes to prayer by its stable, alert tripod solidity. The body's physical stillness facilitates interior stillness, alertness, and calm.

Quietly repeat the prayer word united with the breath. If the prayer word is of more than one syllable or word (such as "Jesus," "Abba," or "Jesus Christ, Son of the living God, have mercy on me"), we inhale on the first syllable (or group of words) and exhale on the second syllable (or group of words). During the time of prayer (normally for periods of at least twenty to twenty-five minutes twice a day), we give our attention entirely to this quiet repetition. Whenever we become aware that we've become distracted, we bring our attention back to the prayer word united to the breath, "continually breathing Jesus Christ."[17]

The basic instruction in the practice of contemplation remains fundamentally the same throughout its seasons of practice: whenever we become aware that our attention has been stolen, we bring it back to the prayer word united with the breath. The practice is not to sit there trying to have no thoughts or only certain thoughts. As St. Teresa of Avila put it centuries ago, "by trying not to think, we hopelessly stimulate the imagination. . . . The harder you try not to think of anything, the more aroused your mind will become and you will think even more."[18] Nor do we push away thoughts in an attempt to generate a dull blankness. Instead we simply bring our attention back to our practice whenever we find that our attention has been stolen. The challenge lies in its simplicity.

The practice of bringing the attention back time and again creates what is called a *habitus* or habit, an interior momentum that gradually excavates the present moment, revealing over time the stillness that is within us all like a buried treasure.

In early seasons of practice there is typically very little sense of our abiding immersion in Silence. Instead, when we try to be silent we find that there is anything but silence. This inner noise is generated by a deeply ingrained tendency, reinforced over a lifetime, to derive our sense of who we are and what our life is about from these thoughts and feelings. We look within and genuinely think that we are our thoughts and feelings. If our thoughts and feelings were a mass of vines and branches, we would say we were smack in the middle of it all. In fact we might even say we were this tangle of vines. Sometimes it seems that it is not our attention that is so easily stolen but that there is a strong headwind that prevents our attention from even focusing on the prayer word. No matter what our experience, the practice remains the same: gently direct the attention back to the prayer word united with the breath. The basic skill we learn at this doorway of practice is to return to the prayer word instead of getting caught up in reactive inner commentary on the distractions.

Because of our nearly complete identification with thoughts, we have a strong tendency to move through life reactively. This generates inner noise and alienates us from the simple experience of thoughts and feelings. Instead we experience reactive commentaries on thoughts and feelings. The ability to meet with stillness all that appears and disappears in awareness will gradually (very gradually) replace this deeply ingrained pattern of meeting experiences with reactive commentary.

The reactive life is strengthened by these sudden spasms of talking, talking, talking, talking to ourselves about life and love and how everybody ought to behave and vote. This twittering chatter keeps the attention riveted to and identified with the objects that appear in our minds. With regular practice and according to timing beyond our control, our practice will begin to change. As our practice deepens, thoughts and feelings continue to come and go, but our relationship with them changes.

"BEHOLD, I STAND AT THE DOOR AND KNOCK" (REV 3:2)

"Delve deeply into the Jesus Prayer," says the Russian monk Theophan.[19] He obviously intends the Jesus Prayer as the prayer word. At an earlier doorway of practice such a statement would have made no sense. We might have recited it, been dedicated to it, been consistent in bringing the attention back, but to "delve deeply into" it would imply that the prayer word had some sort of dimension or depth. This is precisely the sort of change that begins to take place as our contemplative practice matures. Whereas before the prayer word may have seemed something mechanical, constricting, or solid—like butting up against a wall—now the prayer word begins to open up. At this doorway of practice to return to the prayer word is to push off the side of a pool into the deep (Lk 5:4). This depth dimension, a "a breadth without breadth, an expanseless expanse," as Meister Eckhart calls it,[20] is nothing but awareness itself, not an object that we are aware of but the ground of awareness itself. We recognize that the interior spaciousness is somehow deeper even as it embraces and permeates interior and exterior noise (noise that may very well continue to bang on). Whereas before we were caught in reactive commentary that caused us to push away or cling to the thoughts and feelings that come and go, we can now let them be, let them come, go, or stay without attending to them. We let them be because they are. At this doorway of practice we come to discover, perhaps for the first time, that two dynamics characterize the practice of contemplation: deepening concentration and expanding awareness. These two are one. They give birth to twins: inner solitude and a loving solidarity with all, a solidarity that runs deeper than personal preference.

Saint. Isaac the Syrian says, "After a time a certain sweetness is born in the heart out of this practice. Let us give ourselves over to the practice of silence, and then, from out of this silence something is born that leads us into Silence itself."[21] As much a tangle as our practice may seem, it will begin to untangle. One of the signs that our practice is beginning to unfold is that we get a sense of what St. Isaac the Syrian calls "sweetness." Something deeper begins to attract us, and this something deeper is more spacious, alluring, and silent than the tediously dramatic opera scores of inner chatter. The inner chatter will be present, but its grip on our attention loosens. It is as though this mass of thoughts and feelings was a brick wall that once obstructed our vision. But gradually we see that the sense of this wall's solidity is a creation of our identification with these thoughts and feelings. It is not a wall after all but a window. We can actually see through this mass of thoughts into something else in which they are immersed and saturated. This "something else" is untouched and free of all thoughts, even as it suffuses, and permeates, and knows how to do nothing other than be one with all. Something is being born of the practice of silence, and this leads us into Silence itself. As our practice deepens we see that thoughts are as porous as screen, porous to their grounding Silence. Realizing this, we are not quite so compelled to react or push away or grasp. Yet the externals of our practice remain basically the same; whenever we are aware that the attention has been stolen, we bring the attention back, whether or not we need to repeat the prayer word. While the externals of our practice are the same, the practice has become, seemingly of itself, a spacious sort of thing, a place of refuge, indeed a space to move into and out of, a space to be in the midst of however life happens to be at any given moment. This is so even if we find we do not have to repeat the prayer word anymore. At this doorway of practice our relationship with distractions changes.

Whether distractions are tumultuous or tame, this inner spaciousness is able to receive all. Whereas before we may have had a sense of being tight, shallow, and reacting to noise, now we sense that our very awareness itself (not the objects we are aware of, which awareness can never be) is vast, receptive, open, and generous. Receiving and letting go are one and the same. If there is an inner commentary that says, "Oh, wow, look, I'm receiving" or "Look, I'm letting go," we simply meet this and receive it in this flow and are not snagged by this commentary (though that, too, is part of the flow).

What happens at this doorway of practice? Mostly nothing. We simply listen as deeply as Mary to Gabriel (Lk 1:26–38). Our search for God, who has sought and found us from all eternity (Jer 1:5), is shown to be nothing but this deep listening to the alluring knock: "Behold I stand at the door and knock" (Rev 3:2). "I am the Door" (Jn 19:9).

As our practice of silent prayer matures from place of refuge to place of encounter, what is our practice like and what is our relationship with thoughts? The external circumstances of our lives continue to be whatever they happen to be at any given moment, but now we experience these circumstances differently. At the same time we have long begun to take account of and make amends for the many ways in which we set ourselves up for much of our misery by deriving our sense of identity from and acting out of this inner chatter. But the real value of this doorway of practice is that no matter what happens while we are praying, whether miserable or marvelous, we encounter freedom, even in the midst of the reactive chatter about life.

At this doorway of prayer it is often the case that we do not need to repeat the prayer word while praying; an eagle does not always need to flap. With even the simplest impulse to pray (or even when the body happens to adopt its posture of prayer—whether sitting, walking, standing) we are immersed in the luminous expanse of awareness. Moreover this "we" that is immersed in awareness is itself a vast field of awareness that has no boundaries. This form-less vastness bodies forth as prayer.

CONCLUSION

The practice of contemplation quietens the noise that goes on in our heads and allows inner silence to expand. This expanding inner silence is a wide and fertile delta that embraces the mud, reeds, and rushes of all sound, whether delightful or disruptive. Initially, however, the practice of contemplation can strike us as frustratingly awkward, and we react to everything within and without. Though we feel drawn to interior silence, what we find when we turn within is a strong headwind of distractions. There is a characteristic, dominating tendency to identify with these thoughts: we think we are these thoughts and feelings. Thoughts seem to be a solid obstruction to peace to such an extent that we are caught up and pulled right into them. But gradually our practice begins to take root. We learn that our practice is, as the author of *The Cloud of Unknowing* puts it, "to be your shield and your spear,"[22] providing effective protection from the way distractions snag us. Gradually we learn that we are not these thoughts and feelings that come and go any more than we are the weather that comes and goes. We may indeed prefer a certain type of weather, but we are not the weather.

When the prayer word becomes second nature to us, it becomes more than a spear or a shield or a place of refuge: but an endlessly flowing inner spaciousness in which we "live and move and have our being" (Acts 17:28). Therefore, we do not have to flee from our life circumstances or from our thoughts and feelings (yet we are free to if common sense so dictates). These thoughts and feelings are themselves porous to this spacious flow; they, too, manifest the silence we seek. But we do not see this simple fact in the early seasons of practice.

Chattering commentary about our thoughts and feelings, about life in general, creates a sense of obstruction of this flow as well as an inner sense of tight, reactive grip and anxiety. The practice of contemplation gradually loosens this grip, revealing life as luminous flow. Even the thoughts and feelings, which were previously the most distracting obstacles to inner peace, are now seen to be vehicles of it. Distraction is related to the operatic commentary, not to the simple presence or absence of thoughts and feelings.

Whether or not we need to use an explicit prayer word anymore, our practice is simply luminous vastness. What beholds this flowing vastness is also luminous vastness.

The threshold of our own depths leading into Christ's depths is at the same time the threshold of Christ's depths into ours. A single threshold, a single doorway. We move through these doorways, yet each doorway is itself the very fullness that renders our searching useless. The mystery of the God we seek circulates in ever-moving repose through us and in us. Christ reveals God as both door and doorway, both seeker and sought.

For all our striving and attempts to negotiate the riddles and doorways of silence, the practice of contemplation can no more deliver the gift of contemplation than the most skillful sailor can make the wind blow. But without sailing skills the voyage would be reckless. The contemplative, whose skills are trained by the storms and trials of this path, discovers the joy that, while we can never grasp God, God nevertheless does nothing but graciously give to us, ground us, and embrace us. Such is the nature of God's simplicity.

TWO

Our Collection of Videos

They changed their sky but not their souls.
　　　　　—Horace

O Lord you are my rock, my refuge,
Who trains my arms for battle, my fingers
for war.
　　　　　—Psalm 144

Each of us has a soul but we forget to value it.
　　　　　—St. Teresa of Avila

Undergraduates always know exactly what I mean by "mind-tripping" and "inner videos." These terms describe the way a certain thought or train of thoughts quickly steals our attention and sets off a cycle of inner chatter and commentary. This inner chatter is something like a video that constantly plays in the mind only to be rewound and played again and again and again and again. For some it might be a predominantly visual sequence of distractions, for others predominantly aural, or a combination of both. The insidious thing about these videos is that they have a way of cultivating a psychological identification with them. We identify so thoroughly with this chatter that when we attempt to look within, we are actually looking at these videos, and we think "This is my inner life." This mind-tripping state of awareness is nearly always chewing, chattering, and commenting. Moreover, these tape-loops gain a very subtle yet effective momentum. The more we watch or listen to them, the more we identify with them, the more we live out of them and live them out. This is "mind-tripping." It can be tepid or it can be a tempest. It can be entertaining, pious, a horror story, or utterly humdrum. It doesn't really matter. This video, this inner commentary, is nearly always playing, with the result that we are nearly always watching it.

When undergraduates read some of the writings of the fourth-century spiritual writers known as the desert fathers and mothers, they are often surprised to see that this chaos within the mind is a major concern for all who embark on the spiritual path. Evagrius, a fourth-century monk living in Egypt, has perhaps the most to say about these inner videos and how they very subtly keep us from ever embarking on the spiritual path. Students initially respond to Evagrius with bewilderment and reserve. Yet year after year it is Evagrius to whom they warm the most.

Undergraduates today often have a remarkable psychological sensitivity and fragility. It doesn't take them long to see the relevance of distant figures like Evagrius, and they are genuinely intrigued by how, before he became a monk, the life and lifestyle of this immensely talented church careerist suddenly came crashing down as a result of an affair with the wife of a government official.[1] Cryptic as some of his sayings may seem, students perceive in Evagrius a person of deep compassion and insight, a person who understands the struggles they themselves go through because Evagrius, too, has lived them. "I feel like he's been looking inside my journal or something," said one student.

Students will often take writing assignments on Evagrius in a personal direction, as the following examples reveal. Their own words in the following sections serve better than any summary to reveal how much they learn about their own mind-tripping, as their relationship with God develops. Their comments (with sufficient detail changed to protect privacy) have something to teach us all.

"NAY, WORSE THAN STRANGERS"

"We'd been dating for three years." This was the opening sentence of the student's essay on what Evagrius might have to teach undergraduates. He continued:

> She'd met everyone in my family. I even told my parents I thought she might be the one. One day out of the blue my girlfriend said she thought we were "outgrowing our rela-tionship" and that we should stop dating and "just be friends." My world fell apart. When your girlfriend tells you

she just wants to be friends, it means that you'll have lunch maybe a couple of times, then she won't have anything to do with you. We'll be like strangers.

I think I must have been in shock or something, but everything from the moment she said this seemed like it was happening in slow motion. For the next couple of days I just repeated our last conversation over and over again to myself, trying to remember if there was some way I misunderstood her, that she wasn't really breaking it off. Maybe there was something in her voice that suggested she didn't really mean it, that what she really meant was that we just had to work through some issues and then we'd be fine again. She texted me a couple days later. "Let's do lunch tomorrow!" I knew what it would say before I read it. My roommate told me not to go. But like a fool I agreed to meet for lunch the next day.

On the surface she was all bubbles, but underneath it was like being with a perfect stranger. I didn't feel anything. I just felt numb. I just kept going over our last few conversations in my head to see if there was some opening, something that would suggest it wasn't really over. Later that day another friend said he saw her the previous weekend clubbing in Philadelphia with some guy who was in one of her classes. She had told me she was going home to New Jersey that weekend for her sister's wedding shower. When I heard she'd really been at a club with this guy, I decided to drink an entire handle [1.75 litres] of vodka and later had to be taken to the hospital. I don't even drink much. I don't even like vodka.

I couldn't deal with the thought of seeing her with this guy, but it was the *only thing I could think about.* I knew what her class schedule was, when and where she ate, and I would walk ten minutes out of my way just so that I could avoid her in all these likely places. She had class in Bartley Hall just before I did. She always went out the front of the building, so I made sure I always went in the back. For an entire semester I put an incredible amount of energy into making sure I never saw her.

What does Evagrius have to say to people of today? I think his insights into how to deal with all the chaos and confusion and how to cope with fear and pain have a lot to say. But I can say with certainty that I have been helped a great deal.

My contemplative practice is the Jesus Prayer. Of all the forms of the Jesus Prayer, the simple name of Jesus draws me the most. Even from the brief period of time we pray during class I can tell that there is something to this. Our lives as students are so out of control and overprogrammed. To be able to be silent, even briefly, is a refreshing break. I can't do this everyday but most days I did. Usually I'm constantly distracted but once I felt a tremendous peace and warmth coming from deep within me. I'd never experienced anything like that before. It lasted most of the day then went away. But it had a lasting effect. I felt more drawn to that place within that I didn't know was there, and it was easier to return there, much easier. The distractions in my head weren't as strong.

But now that this has happened with my girlfriend (or former girlfriend), it's impossible to pray. I'm afraid of silence now. There's too much anger and hurt and probably a lot more that I don't know about. Evagrius says, "When the spirit begins to be free from all distractions, then there begins an all-out battle day and night against the irascible part."[2] This is exactly what happened. To pray is now a battle. I wouldn't say that I was ever free from distractions, but there had been this warming sensation all over and peacefulness and a growing sense that the Jesus Prayer was an anchor or some sort of opening. Now there is this panic and pain and anger. Apart from the time we take in class to practice contemplation, time for prayer just isn't going to happen. Evagrius says, "The fact is that this demon entertains the hope of causing us to cease to pray."[3] He's certainly right there. I also think Evagrius is right when he says that "resentment blinds the reason of the one who prays and casts a cloud over his prayer."[4] Drinking a handle of vodka made absolutely no sense.

My friends told me I had a right to be angry because she had cheated on me. But I've always been very emotional.

My problem isn't being in touch with my feelings. The more I would act out my anger, the angrier I would get. At first it was very helpful to talk about it, but soon the more I talked about it the more I would mind-trip on the anger. Evagrius says that "such matters come to mind as would seem clearly to justify your getting angry."[5] "If you restrain your anger you yourself will be spared."[6] There is a difference between feeling anger, just letting it be, and acting it out (sometimes in stupid ways that land you in the hospital). Sometimes I think acting it out strengthens it. Evagrius says, "Anger and hatred increase anger."[7] This is something the Jesus Prayer can be very helpful for. Just say the Jesus Prayer in the middle of the anger. Evagrius says, "At times just as soon as you rise you pray well. At other times, work as you may, you achieve nothing. But this happens so that by seeking still more intently, and then finally reaching the mark, you may possess your prize without fear of loss."[8] I think Evagrius is saying that it's just as important to pray in the midst of difficulty as it is to pray when things are OK. With the Jesus Prayer you can do this.

This young man later reported that he did in fact "see her with this guy." And as he had predicted, they were like strangers. "Now they were as strangers; nay, worse than strangers," but unlike Captain Wentworth and Anne Elliot in Jane Austen's *Persuasion*, there was no prospect of a second chance.[9]

BLIND WITH ANGER

Evagrius helped lead another student into liberating insight into the nature of her very active mind, especially the connection between her anger and her fear. While she was less revealing of the details of her struggles, she was grappling with the fallout and follow-through of an intervention initiated by concerned friends. She admits it needed to be done but she still struggles with feelings of betrayal and more. She wrote:

> Evagrius seems to know that as much as our mind-tripping on inner videos causes suffering, we somehow find them fascinating and so we have to be careful. He says the demons use vivid images for this combat, "and we run to see them."[10] Intellectually I understood that my friends were trying to help me. But the *thought* that they betrayed me gets me mind-tripping on self-pity, and I almost always just go with it. If I can see myself as being a victim, I can more easily stay in denial of the issues that concerned my friends. In a weird sort of way being this victim was more comforting than the fact that my behavior was making me ill and that my friends thought

they needed to let someone know. I can see that I do this. This mind-tripping, what Evagrius calls "passions" stirred up by a thought or image, can actually make us sick. Not just spiritually, but mentally and physically as well. If we're not careful, he says, "under the influence of this part of our soul, we then grow unhealthy while our passions undergo a full-bodied development."[11] Anger, resentment, self-pity can even make you completely crazy: "Those who long for true prayer but are given over to anger or resentment will be beside themselves with madness. They are like someone who wants to see clearly but keeps scratching her eyes."[12] I don't know if Evagrius came up with the phrase "blind with anger," but he basically says it: "Resentment blinds the reason of one who prays and casts a cloud over prayer."[13] Blinded as I may be by my anger, all this mind-tripping seems very real at the time. Evagrius says, "These things are depicted vividly before our eyes."[14] "The most fierce passion is anger. . . . It constantly irritates the soul and above all at the time of prayer it seizes the mind and flashes the picture of the offensive person before one's eyes."[15] The purpose of all this mind-tripping is to keep us from going deeper within where God dwells, "to cease to pray so that we might not stand in the presence of the Lord our God, not dare to raise our hands in supplication to one against whom we have had such frightful thoughts."[16]

Another thing that Evagrius has taught me is how closely related are anger, fear, and pain. The more fear, the more anger. Evagrius seems to say this. He defines anger as "a boiling up and stirring up of wrath against one who has given injury."[17] I found this statement very helpful. I always thought of my anger as a response to something or someone who had offended me. But Evagrius suggests that anger is a response to pain, to being hurt. If I learn how to handle pain better, I might learn how to handle anger better. But what I find most helpful is the link he establishes between anger and fear. I have recently realized that anger and fear are very closely related. In psychology class we learned about the fight/flight response. But Evagrius sees that anger can sow the seeds of fear or can somehow turn into fear: "Images of a frightful kind usually arise from anger's disturbing influence."[18] I've always known that I struggle a lot with fear but have only recently come to see that when I'm very angry, I will wake up afraid.

In the abstract, "spirituality" may sound especially attractive nowadays, when it is not only quite trendy but can also be supported by over-the-counter supplements that are sure to work synergistically with it. But embarking on any spiritual path will soon involve us in an interior battle, a battle "fought on the field of thought more severe than that which is conducted in the arena of things and events."[19] The problem is the noise in our heads. This is why the great spiritual masters offer practical advice on how to deal with our reactions to our thoughts and feelings. For *reacting* to them generates the inner video. This inner video can become our predominant experience of inner life.

CLINGING TO DISTRACTION LIKE
A DOG TO A BONE

Evagrius and others have a psychological description of how these inner videos are generated. There is within us a sort of mental craving that is fragmented and frayed (*pathos* was the Greek word he often used), with the result that we are nearly always either grasping at something or pushing it away and find it very difficult to receive with open palms of simple gratitude.

What happens when this mental craving grasps some thought or image? The videos are produced, and "we run to see them."[20] Saint Hesychios says, "As soon as this thought appears in our intellect, our thoughts chase after it and become embroiled with it."[21] It should not be underestimated how quickly this happens. You can be perfectly content with your Mac Powerbook. *This is it!* It's everything you could want in a computer. Then the MacBook appears and suddenly, *This is it!* It's everything you could want in a computer.

And so you massage your budget to manage this purchase. Now you've just seen MacBook Air. *This is it!* Such simplicity of line. It fits into a manila envelope. It's everything you could want in a computer. So it goes. And we find ourselves returning to the Apple store like a dog to a fire hydrant.

Analysis of the lightning-quick subtleties of chatter-fueled distraction and its ability to split, fray, and knot desire is typical of the desert psychology of the early Christian centuries. Though the language and perspective may at times seem dated, the dynamics are strikingly accurate. Someone, for example, turns down your invitation to dinner, and immediately a stream of inner commentary breaks loose: "They don't like me I suppose. *Nobody* likes me. I've never had any true friends in my *whole* life. *Not ever.* I'll *never* ask anybody over *again*." Somebody walks into a room carrying a Gucci bag that you yourself cannot afford but crave nonetheless, and immediately the mind comments, "Doesn't she look silly carrying that thing? Just look at her! What on *earth* does she think she's doing with *that*?" The inner chatter is not only concerned with silly things; it can generate quite a lot of suffering. This suffering requires mental noise to make it seem real. And soon we've given it the keys to the car.

Mental craving acts like a whisk that quickly froths things up into foamy obsession. Evagrius famously says in his *Praktikos* that this can happen in one of eight ways (or a combination thereof). The eight afflictive thoughts are gluttony, impurity, avarice, sadness, anger, acedia, vainglory, and pride.[22] In other writings he mentions anxiety, envy, judgmentalism, and resentment as well.[23] It is never a question of somehow managing never to have any of these kinds of thoughts. It is subtler than that. Evagrius is suggesting that there are certain areas of life where obsessive patterns tend to occur. Some pertain to more basic things, such as anxiety over our material welfare (gluttony or avarice, for example), while others pertain to a more rational dimension, such as anxiety over what people think of us (vainglory). He pinpoints certain areas of life in which inner noise, anxiety, confusion are frothed up by the mind's whisk with the result that we become out of touch with reality. If we are out of touch with reality, we are at the same time out of touch with ourselves, with others, and with God.

Evagrius sees our relationship with food to be one such area, but it has much more to do than merely with what we eat. If we think for a moment how obsessed our culture is with how our bodies appear to others, this does not seem so far-fetched. And when our life coaches and personal trainers shore up their salaries by telling us how good we look, the nostrils of our gratitude flare condescendingly at all those mountainously overweight people. "Haven't they ever looked in a mirror?" we ask ourselves. It is easy to see what

Evagrius is getting at when he says these afflictive thoughts can team up with each other.

In her memoir of her battle with an eating disorder, Margaret Bullet-Jonas recounts how bulimia ushered her into a world of chaotic fragmentation in order to illustrate the crippling isolation of mind-tripping gone out of control. "The language of compulsive overeating," she writes,

> is tragically jumbled and ineffective, as multitoned and multivoiced as Cerberus, the dog who stands at the threshold of hell in Greek mythology, each of its three heads barking independently. A person who stands at the brink of addictive behavior is listening intently to conflicting inner voices. . . . It would all begin with a small seductive voice that made promises it couldn't keep. "Here, I'll take care of you," it would murmur in my ear. "I see you're feeling a bit down. Let's just comfort ourselves with a bite to eat, shall we?"
>
> "Oh no, not again," another inner voice would object in alarm. "I'm not going to eat right now. . . . "
>
> "Hey, you don't have to feel that sadness. Don't give in to it. Leave it alone. Come with me. Let's go see what's in the pantry. Just a little something to eat, that's all you need."[24]

A student in one class who, due to bipolar disorder, struggled more than most with inner chatter, knew this cacophony well, and reminded the class one day that Cerberus guards the door not only to keep people from entering but also to keep people from leaving. The noise generated by our inner commentaries, many of them hidden, heightens the sense of isolation and inhibits the ability to reach out to others.

What is wrong with scratching the thighs of our inner chatter until they are reddened, chapped, or torn by bitten fingernails of obsession? Whether scratching the thighs of resentment, anguish, old pain, or simply chewing the cud of all the silly cartoons that bounce around in our heads, surely this constant talking, talking, talking to ourselves is perfectly normal. Yes, it is normal, if we call normal a lifetime of believing we are separate from God. This is what most of us experience much of the time. Yet this utterly convincing, self-alienating sense of reactive separation from God is precisely what interior noise generates and sustains.

Though addressing monks in his own monastery, St. Hesychios speaks to all of us on the contemplative path when he says, "One who has renounced such things as marriage, possessions and other worldly pursuits is outwardly a monk, but may not be a monk inwardly. Only the person who has renounced obsessive thoughts is a true monk."[25] For Hesychios, then, a monk is not a geriatric vegetarian who mutters prayers, but any woman or man who seeks to become one, single person (the root meaning of "monk"),[26] instead of the chameleon who constantly changes according to the color of demanding relationships. The single-hearted search for God requires this renunciation of obsessive thoughts, our video collection.

Saint Theodoros speaks similarly when he equates monastic withdrawal from the world with this world of mind-tripping: "Withdrawal from the world means two things: the withering away of our obsessions and the revelation of the life that is hidden in Christ."[27] It is not ultimately a question of embracing the externals of monasticism. We may go off to retreat houses or enter a monastery, but unless we quieten the world of inner chatter, we *never* enter. Countless numbers of monastics may live decades in a monastery without ever entering the monastery in the sense St. Hesychios or St. Theodoros intends, because we cling to chatter like a dog to a bone. Saint Basil the Great realizes this when he himself goes off to found his own monastery. He writes to his friend St. Gregory of Nazianzus, "I am ashamed to write what I myself do night and day in this out-of-the-way place. For I have indeed left my life in the city . . . but I have not yet been able to leave myself behind. . . . For we carry our indwelling disorders about within us, and so are nowhere free from the same sort of disturbances. Consequently we have derived no great benefit from our present solitude."[28] All the noise of his mental craving went into the monastery with him. As Horace observed of many, "they changed their sky but not their soul."[29] The only monastery we all need to enter is the one Jesus opened up as he disclosed the inner depths of his own identity and purpose: "I and the Father are one" (Jn 10:30).

The world of our videos is the worldliness we are supposed to leave, but instead "we run to see them."[30] Why do we need to leave behind our collection of videos? Because they deafen the listening heart. As St. Augustine puts it with insight born of experience, "All the time I wanted to stand and listen. To listen to Your voice. But I could not, because another voice, the voice of my ego, dragged me away."[31]

We might well wonder, Am I somehow at fault for having all these distractions? The wisdom of the desert takes a rather practical approach to this question. It is not in our control whether these videos play: "It is not in our power to determine whether we are disturbed by these thoughts," says Evagrius.[32] However, this does not mean we have no recourse but to be chained as prisoners in the cave of this cinema for the rest of our days. Evagrius insists that "it is up to us to decide if they are to linger within us or not and whether or not they are to stir up our obsessions."[33] If met correctly, that is, with stillness and not commentary, they end up providing a valuable contribution to our training in the spiritual arts of awareness and stillness. As the distance runner does not grow in strength and endurance without a challenging terrain, or the pianist in stamina and skill without a challenging score, neither does the person of prayer deepen in freedom, wisdom, and compassion without these trials. As St. Isaac of Nineveh puts it, "Without temptations, God's concern is not perceived, nor is freedom of speech with him acquired, nor is spiritual wisdom learnt, nor does the love of God become grounded in the soul."[34]

Whether we live in a monastery or not, the grip our inner videos have on us must be loosened. Awareness and stillness are the skills we cultivate to allow this to take place. The result is that our minds will be clearer and more silent.

One of the most debilitating results of the spiritual fragmentation that has plagued Christianity in the last several centuries has been the opposition of the contemplative life to the active life. Both individuals and communities happily enjoy this schizophrenia. One of the early realizations of the life of stillness is that the opposite of the contemplative life is not the active life but the *reactive* life: highly habituated emotional styles and lifestyles that keep us constantly reacting to life like victimizing victims, ever more convinced that the videos that dominate and shape our awareness are in fact true. The life of stillness gradually heals this split and leads us into wide-open fields where buried treasure lies (Mt 13:45–46), fields where the soul can "bathe in its own space" and "make long swathes in meadow lengths of space."[35] The God we seek already shines through our eyes. May our seeking not blind us to what already lies "hidden in plain sight all around us."[36]

THREE

The Open Porches of the Mind

On Silence and Noise

The result of justice will be silence and trust forever.
—Isaiah 32:17

Let stillness be the criterion for assessing everything.
—Evagrius

If you love truth, love silence.
—Isaac the Syrian

THE BLACKBIRD SINGING

With hopes of teaching them all how to draw, Kathleen Norris stands before her classroom of elementary school students. She recounts in *Amazing Grace* her remarkable way of going about this. Before teaching them to draw, she first needs to teach them how to be silent and aware. She explains to the class that when she raises her hand they are to make as much noise as they possibly can, but when she lowers her hand, they must all be completely silent. No noise, no movement, no making funny faces. The lesson begins: she raises her hand, and an almighty racket ensues. But as soon as she drops her hand the noise indeed stops instantly. They were "so still," she says, "that silence became a

presence in the classroom." What fascinates Norris most is how
the "silence liberated the imagination of so many children."[1] Her
simple exercise with these school children shows us something
important about the nature of silence. Silence is not simply
about the absence of sound waves. It is concerned with attention
and awareness. Silence and awareness are in fact one thing.

Poets seem to know about this unity of silence and awareness. Wallace Stevens shows this in his "Thirteen Ways of
Looking at a Blackbird":

> I do not know which to prefer,
> The beauty of inflections
> Or the beauty of innuendoes,
> The blackbird whistling
> Or just after.[2]

The song of the blackbird evokes the same attentive wonder
as when the blackbird stops singing. Robert Penn Warren
likewise perceives the porous union of sound and silence, in
his famous poem "The Enclave":

> Out of the silence, the saying. Into
> The silence, the said. Thus
> Silence, in timelessness, gives forth
> Time, and receives it again, and I lie
> In darkness and hear the wind off the sea heave.[3]

As vital as physical silence is for opening up the depth of the present moment, silence does much more than simply tiptoe around; its essence has little to do with the absence of sound waves. For Silence has no opposite. Its embrace is wide and generous enough to receive all, both sound and the absence of sound. The practice of contemplation gradually reveals the Silent Presence flowing through the mud and reeds and rushes of both noise and sound.

Without doubt, regular periods of physical silence play a crucial role in the spiritual life. It must be cultivated and reverenced. We don't make retreats alongside highways. Places of retreat, centers of recovery and healing, even some religious communities purposely cultivate physical silence in service of something else. Stretches of physical silence and contemplation, especially on a daily basis, help destress the nervous system.[4] While the constant stimulation of the noise of everyday life keeps anxiety levels high and our attention fixed on objects that we are (more or less) aware of, whether an exterior object such as a computer screen or an interior object such as a thought or feeling or mind-tripping inner video. But God is not an object in the way these things are objects and therefore cannot be an object of our awareness in the same way. This is one of the implications of what theology calls the Divine Simplicity. All creation emerges from and points to (at one and the same time) this simple, grounding Source that is not a particular thing in the way creatures are. An environment of physical simplicity and silence helps relax the tight grip of our mind's reactive preoccupation with objects in order that deeper ways of encountering God, which we all have within us, may emerge and open and receive that Light that constantly gives and sustains all that is.

SOME VARIETIES OF SILENCE

Not all silence is the same. There is the awkward silence of the road trip with someone we do not know quite well enough to be silent next to, the refrigerating silence of hardened anger, the reverential silence of dogwoods in winter, the vast silence of a cathedral, the focused silence of absorption in our sewing or a good book, the stunned silence of seeing the status of our pension fund. Each features physical silence, the absence of sound waves, but this silence is merely the outer form of other dynamics. In the spiritual life silence is characterized by a powerfully searching and subtle dynamic. If we know how to dwell in physical silence, then silence becomes not a threat but attractive, nurturing, and liberating.

The powerful attraction of something as utterly simple as silence is well attested throughout the contemplative tradition. The following is a good example of how silence is not simply concerned with a buttoned lip or a cold shoulder. The fourteenth-century Augustinian friar and spiritual writer

Jordan of Saxony not only shaped the spirituality of his own religious community but also stood on the shoulders of countless saints and sages who have witnessed to what silence does other than make no noise. He presumes that any community that seeks God together is going to have places where "silence should be observed. From this silence peace of mind is born, advance in studies is promoted, devout contemplation takes its beginnings; furthermore, according to the words of the prophet: 'the cultivation of justice is silence' (Is 32:17); through silence a brother begins to cultivate and practice justice, by which virtue he is formed so as to live his own life honestly, not to harm others, and to give each one his due. Such formation as this carries anyone so formed on to the state of perfection. On the other hand, from the breakdown of silence disturbances of mind arise . . . quarrels are born, strife."[5]

Notice all the things silence does other than be quiet. Silence is real enough to be afraid of. But when integrated into an environment and a way of living, it calms and gradually integrates us into it. Jordan of Saxony sees the generative power of silence; its children are "peace of mind" and "the cultivation of justice." This peace is not the opposite of turmoil but the ground of both turmoil and tranquility. Moreover, silence is formative and developmental; it leads us to "perfection," that is to say, it draws us to completion or wholeness. The breakdown of silence (environmental, generative, or developmental) has dire consequences: an increase in anxiety and quarrels, which fuels the sense of alienation from ourselves, from God, and from those with whom we live. Like many spiritual masters before and after him, Jordan of Saxony knows the cost of the loss of silence in one's living environment and in one's prayer life. The twentieth-century Swiss psychoanalyst C. G. Jung apparently knew this, and today medicine has discovered the practice of contemplation to be an effective destressor, with direct bearing on weight control, blood pressure, and much more.[6]

There is a story told of how Jung used silence to help one of his patients become aware of the cause of his problems. Complaining of a general anxiety, but unable to identify what he was anxious about, the client did not give Jung much to work with. Jung suggested he go home and spend the evenings alone and see what came up before their next appointment the following week. The man returned and told Jung that he had enjoyed the evenings alone at home; he had read a novel he had been meaning to read for months and listened to symphonies he had not enjoyed for years. Jung said, "Ah! I didn't mean go home and read or listen to music just now. I meant go home during the evenings and just be silent." And so the man went home and did just that. When he returned the following week he had plenty that he could begin to talk about. The silence had begun to draw out some of the problems that underlay this man's anxiety so that he could now begin to address them. Silence is sometimes like a poultice placed over a sore to draw out infection as part of the healing process.

THE SILENCE OF THE ELECTRIC SAW

It is one thing to see the unity of silence and sound when our teachers are birdsong and the sea's breaking waves. But what might Wallace Stevens or Robert Penn Warren say about unpleasant noise? Can noise also be a vehicle of that "peace after perfect speech"? Does the sound we would prefer *not* to hear have anything to reveal? Can noise, too, be a teacher pointing to the Silence that is the ground of all? Is noise also (like everything else that exists) a spoke leading into the hub that is the Center of us all?[7]

The measure of our ability to live in silence is our reaction to noise (whether external or internal) and not the length of time we go without hearing anything or hearing only what we like to hear. As contemplative practice matures, we begin to relate to disruptive noise differently. We learn to meet sound that displeases with the same stillness with which we meet the sounds that please us, as the following account reveals.

Gareth had been drawn and dedicated to the practice of contemplation over many years. He heard about a week-long retreat on contemplative prayer and thought this would be a good way to deepen his prayer life. The small retreat house was situated in a mountain village that overlooked a valley. The silence that pervaded the whole place was indescribable, and he settled easily into the spirit of the retreat along with all the other retreatants. They all sat together in silent prayer for a total of about seven hours spread throughout the course of the day. They combined this with manual work as well as some free time for napping or walks in nature. The retreat ended up being a pivotal breakthrough for him, not because of the prayerful silence and beauty of the mountains but because of the outrageously annoying buzz of an electric saw.

For about an hour in the afternoon over three consecutive days, the neighbor next door to the retreat house would saw timber with his electric table saw. Gareth thought his fillings were going to vibrate out of his back teeth, and he seriously considered either skipping that period of prayer or simply returning home. He just could not believe that this sort of disruption was happening during his retreat. The retreat guide advised him just to stick with it and to use the ordeal as an experiment in cultivating interior stillness in the midst of irritating noise. Apart from this hour there was virtually complete absence of irritating noise. To the retreat guide's amazement, Gareth decided to try to adopt a mature attitude and follow this advice. He ended up discovering something important about silence.

Coping with disruptive noise that we simply cannot do anything about does not so much call for praying to the patron saint of noise reduction as for being resolved that it's okay for the noise to be there if it happens to be there and nothing can be done about it. To get caught up in a buzzing commentary on how irritating the noise is makes for a noisy relationship with noise. The irritation is something the mind adds. We need a simpler relationship with noise. Instead of meeting an irritating buzz saw, we just want to let the buzz saw be there if nothing can be done about it. For this to happen, two things are required.

First, if our practice has been deeply established, we are in a position to learn something from silence and its generous way of allowing noise to be present when it happens to be present. To get caught up in commentary on the noise will not make it go away but will only tighten the clenching of our jaws around our preference that the noise be gone. Our own generous release into our practice mirrors what silence does all the time; silence is wide and gracious enough to allow sound, even irritating sound, to be present. Second, instead of trying to push disruption away, we shift our attention away from the disrupting noise to our prayer word or to whatever our contemplative practice is. The return is not a pushing away or a reactive clinging, but a generous release into our practice. We will soon begin to see that the noisy disruptions that we cannot control become an exercise, a training, that strengthens us in our practice, the way a challenging terrain strengthens the distance runner. But again this return to our practice will not be a pushing away or a flight from the disruption. Deepening immersion in contemplative practice is simultaneous with allowing the disruption to be present; we just become better at not letting it steal our attention. And when it inevitably does, we simply bring the attention home without comment. This is what Gareth needed to learn.

He preferred to have no disturbance. But through a gift of insight he saw that the silence was actually receiving the sound of the saw, and he released himself into his practice instead of reacting to the irritating noise. He let the sound be, simply because it was. He could soon see that the sound of the saw was simply the sound of the saw. The sense of irritation was supplied by mental commentary.

Gareth's inability to cope with the sound of the electric saw disrupting a contemplative prayer retreat resulted from his spasms of preference for only sounds that pleased him, such as birdsong, the rustling of leaves, or rain. Apart from his inner contortions during this one hour of outrageous disruption, there was nothing else going on just then except a saw making the sound saws make when they're switched on and sawing through timber. The more he allowed the noise to be present, without fighting the fact that it was there, the more he could simply sit in the midst of it. He would have preferred, and with good reason, that the noise not be there (and ideally it should not have been), but he was amazed that, after this deepened release into his practice, his mind no longer hopped around like drops of oil on a hot skillet.

Gareth's breakthrough came when he was sitting there during a period of silent prayer as the electric saw squealed. He said later to the retreat guide, "I do not know how to put this into words. My commenting mind simply fell way. There was only the sound of the saw, but there was no commenting mind listening to it. There was only the sound of a saw. Now that this is in the past, and I reflect upon it, it sounds silly. But I know that when the mind is still, sound is as silent as no sound."

Gareth's experience was a real grace but should not be considered exceptional to the dynamics of inner silencing. Saint Isaac the Syrian says, "Love silence above all things, because it brings you near to the fruit that the tongue cannot express."[8] He encourages us to practice silence diligently; "then, from out of this silence something is born that leads to Silence itself."[9]

Meister Eckhart says, "The noblest attainment in this life is to be silent."[10] By "silent" does this fourteenth-century Dominican friar simply mean physical silence? He means far more than this and calls it being "in the right state of mind." Eckhart illustrates this in a provocative way in an address to young people who are training to be fellow members of his Dominican Order. In characteristic fashion, Eckhart shocks his audience a bit. He says, "I was once asked: 'Some people like to withdraw from company and prefer always to be alone. That is where they find peace. . . . Is this the best thing?' My answer was 'No'!"[11] Why would Eckhart say "No"? He is fully aware that physical silence is the preferred environment for prayer and that it needs to be valued and cultivated. But deep prayer is not about a physically silent environment, but about the Loving Communion that is Silence itself, and Silence itself is deeper than the presence or absence of sound waves. A silent environment is the opposite of a noisy environment, but the Silence Eckhart wants to lead these students to has no opposite. It grounds all that appears and disappears in awareness, all that comes and goes. Eckhart is trying to nudge his audience toward this discovery. The realization of this silence that has no opposite is what he calls being in "the right state of mind." This "right state of mind" is a silent mind and is always present within us. Therefore, Eckhart says, "if he is in the right state of mind he is so whether he is in church or the market place."[12] Gareth made good use of what disrupting noise had to teach him.

Not all the retreatants had the same breakthrough Gareth had. On the second to last day of the retreat, as soon as the neighbor's table saw began its daily squeal, one man got up from his place in the oratory, stormed out of the retreat center, and rampaged over to the neighbor's garage. He then yanked the saw's electric cord out of its socket, overturned the neighbor's table saw, and shouted at a volume all could hear, "What in the name of God do you think you're doing sawing wood when all these people have paid good money to have a week's peace and quiet?" A brief interchange between the two men ensued. The level of language was not especially elevated. But the saw ceased its daily hour of buzzing squeal, and for what was left of the retreat the only sound was birdsong, the mooing of distant cattle, rainfall, and the "sound of a gentle breeze" (1 Kgs 19:12). We each make our way on the pathless path of contemplation along different trails, each trail thick with tangled vines of Providence.

A WHEEL FULL OF SPOKES

Indeed silence does more than tiptoe around the house. Silence moves through all sound like water through netting. The deeper our own interior silence, the more we take on its gracious ways of opening up the tight mind that clenches its teeth around what it wants and spits out what it doesn't want.

The optimal environment for prayer is physical silence. Saint Augustine, surely one of the most eloquent people in history, thought it was better to keep silent than to speak and that "one should speak only if it is a duty demanded by one's office." He continues, "Why do you want to speak and not want to listen? You are always rushing out of doors but are unwilling to return into your own house. Your teacher is within."[13] Physical silence is good for us and needs to be pursued, cultivated, understood, and revered. Physical silence increases our awareness of all that is going on around us, especially the needs and sensitivities of others. Luis de León, O.S.A., the sixteenth-century Spanish Augustinian friar and lyric poet, extols the value of physical silence in his poem "The Quiet Life": how peaceful is the life, he says,

> of him who would all worldly clamour shun
> and take the hidden path
> whereon have walked alone
> those few wise men the world has ever known.[14]

But not too far down the spiritual path we learn that there is a deeper silence that does not require sound waves to be gone.

For the mind that is silent, noise is as direct a spoke into the hub of silence as are birdsong, wind, and waves. It requires nothing more than to meet noise with stillness and not commentary. This is easier said than done and comes after many seasons of practice and much failure. But whether the noise in question is an electric table saw, rush-hour traffic, heavy-footed neighbors in the apartment above us, difficult life circumstances at home or work or, more deafening, the mind-numbing din of the cocktail party in our heads, the way of silence receives with engaged awareness all that is, just as it is, as a large screened-in porch receives whatever breeze that blows. R. S. Thomas prays that silence may work on us "so those closed porches be opened once more . . . for the better ventilating of the atmosphere of the closed mind."[15] Silence circulates through the open porches of the mind. But to the mind unventilated by silence, there is only what we like and what we dislike coming at us from all sides, day after day, indeed decade after decade.

Life has a way of being exactly the way it happens to be at any given moment. Life-being-how-it-is (just this) is a wheel of spokes leading into the hub of Silence, irrespective of the presence or absence of pleasant or unpleasant sound. Surely we have our preference as to sound or absence of sound, but Silence resounds in all sound, pleasant or unpleasant. This Silence resounding in all sound ventilates the porches of the mind and makes the ears of attention attend. Discovering the Silence that resounds in all sound, even in noise, places us in what Meister Eckhart calls "the right state of mind," whether we are in country quiet or market mayhem. This strengthens our practice of contemplation.

FOUR

A Sunlit Absence

The Light of Awareness

This light itself is one, and all those who see
it and love it are one.
—St. Augustine

The center of our soul is difficult to define. It's hard enough
just to believe in it.
—St. Teresa of Avila

Because it is not I who look
but I who am being looked through, Gloria.
—R. S. Thomas

GALLERY OF LIGHT

People visit the Academy in Florence mostly to see Michelangelo's *David*. The postcards and the photographs in coffee-table books simply do not reveal his corporeal dignity. *David* presides at the end of a long gallery, where he bodies forth an intelligence inscrutably luminous and spacious.

Easily eclipsed by *David*'s splendor is a less famous series of sculptures by Michelangelo called *Slaves*. They slot in along the side of the gallery. At first they snag the attention more than command it. In contrast to *David*'s shining prowess and preening sheen, they are rough and unfinished. Worry-worn and crumbling in despair of ever stepping free of the shackling stone, they remain forever incomplete.

According to ancient theory of art, the practice of sculpting has less to do with fashioning a figure of one's choosing than with being able to see in the stone the figure waiting to be liberated. The sculptor imposes nothing but only frees what is held captive in stone. The practice of contemplation is something like this. It does not work by means of addition or acquisition, but by release, chiseling away thought-shackled illusions of separation from God. We emerge from the debris of separation and stand up, "set free from the snare of the fowler" (Ps 91:3). The third-century spiritual master Plotinus speaks of contemplation and sculpture in his treatise "On Beauty": "If you do not find yourself beautiful yet," he advises, "act as does the creator of a statue that is to be made beautiful: he cuts away here, he smoothes there, he makes this line lighter, this other purer, until a lovely face has grown upon his work. So do you also, cut away all that is excessive, straighten all that is crooked, bring light to all that is overcast, labour to make all one glow of beauty and never cease chiselling your statue, until there shall shine out on you from it the godlike splendour of virtue."[1] The Orthodox monk Amphilochios of Patmos proclaims, "You should be joyful! Jesus holds a chisel in his hands. He wants to make you into a statue for the heavenly place."[2] Saint Teresa of Avila describes this process with a more succulent metaphor; she likens it to peeling fruit. "Imagine a palmetto fruit. Layer upon layer must be peeled away to reach the tasty part in the middle."[3]

If God is the sculptor, our practice is like a chisel that works effectively and patiently to remove stone. Just as the progress of chiseling, brushing, and blowing away debris and dust is not by way of acquisition, the way an assembly of bricks and mortar acquires us a building, so the practice of contemplation does not acquire for us some *thing*. Contemplative practice proceeds by way of the engaged receptivity of release, of prying loose, of letting go of the need to have our life circumstances be a certain way in order for us to live or pray or be deeply happy.

The stone that is removed is our embedded and frenzied preoccupation with the inner video and all the ego-metrics involved in trying to gauge just how our spiritual lives are progressing. With enough of this stone removed, the chiseling becomes a quiet excavation of the present moment. What emerges from the chiseled and richly veined poverty of the present moment? The emerging figure is our life as Christ (Phil 1:21; Col 3:3–4).

Saint Augustine says, "Therefore, brothers and sisters, what calls for all our efforts in this life is the healing of the eye of the heart, with which God is to be seen."[4] What does this inner eye see once it is restored to health? Many of the saints and sages of the contemplative tradition speak of this restoration in a language of vastness, light, awareness, and watchfulness. At the beginning of *The Interior Castle*, St. Teresa of Avila, for example, insists that "The soul is vast, spacious, plentiful. This amplitude is impossible to exaggerate. . . . The sun at the center of this place radiates to every part."[5] By the book's end she is still speaking of our depths along these lines, "We are not referring to some dark corner, but to a vast inner space."[6] According to St. Augustine, this vast inner space of the soul, an "abyss" as he terms it, is completely open and porous to God: "Indeed, Lord, to your eyes, the abyss of human consciousness is naked."[7]

This spaciousness describes not only *David* in his gallery of light but also the inner eye that perceives the gallery of light. Awareness, consciousness, watchfulness is this vast inner space, radiating everywhere. It is not an object; rather, all objects (physical objects or internal objects like thoughts and feelings) appear and disappear in this awareness, a "sunlit absence," to adapt Seamus Heaney.[8] Always luminous but never quite pinned down, this sunlit absence suffuses and embraces all, as open to the Luminous Ground as air to light. "In your light, Lord, we see light" (Ps 36:10).

AWARENESS: SILENCE'S VERY OWN PRACTICE

The practice of contemplation over many winters into spring often leads to a subtle but fundamental shift in prayer: from using a prayer word as a means of concentration to simple sitting in awareness. Just being. It is much as St. John of the Cross describes it: "Preserve a loving attentiveness to God with no desire to feel or understand any particular thing concerning God."[9] When inner silence sits in simple repose, its prayer is naked awareness. If we used a prayer word, it has not disappeared so much as opened up, something like the way a tulip opens up: what was tightly gathered in pointed focus begins to swell, expand, and open. And now this pollen-painted bowl of petals holds air and light-filled emptiness. This is awareness.

Saint Hesychios, and many like him, consider awareness to define contemplative practice. "Awareness is a spiritual method which, sedulously practiced over a long period, completely frees us with God's help from compulsive thoughts."[10] It "activates" the soul, enabling us "to penetrate the divine and hidden mysteries," and "leads us, insofar as this is possible, to a sure knowledge of the inapprehensible God."[11] Once it is established, and this comes only with time, "it guides us to a true and holy way of life."[12] Addressing these words to his brother monks, St. Hesychios cannot overlook the opportunity to remark: "it is now rather rare among monks."[13]

The practice of awareness has an invaluable potential. As it moves from bud to flower to fruit, awareness is not merely an awareness of particular things (though this is by no means reduced), but a ripening, an opening up from within awareness, an opening up that both grounds and

embraces our *awareness of* this or that thing. Silence cultivates awareness, and when cultivated sufficiently, awareness opens up in the Depths in which we are immersed and
have always been immersed. But this realization of what
has always been the case does not usually happen all at once,
any more than a tree moves from seed to sapling and
branch, without seasons of interaction with the soil, water,
and light of our daily lives.

Saint Hesychios identifies three moments in this process
in which awareness becomes increasingly ungrasping,
expansive, and luminous. "While we are being strengthened in Christ Jesus and beginning to move forward in
steadfast watchfulness, He at first appears in our intellect
like a torch which, when grasped by the hand of the intellect, guides us along the tracks of the mind; then He appears
to us like a full moon, circling the heart's firmament; then
He appears to us like the sun, radiating justice, clearly
revealing Himself in the full light of spiritual vision."[14]

The whole human software and circuitry of interiority
that St. Hesychios calls "intellect" has little to do with book
smarts or formal education. The wherewithal of human
interiority to negotiate the spiritual journey runs deep.
Awareness itself runs deep and communes with the Sacred
like the Hudson River meeting the Atlantic. The Hudson
flows a hundred miles into the Atlantic, while the Atlantic
reaches into the freshwaters of the Hudson up as far as

Newburgh, New York.[15] This type of union between waters is something St. Teresa of Avila herself finds useful in explaining the union between the soul and God. She says union with God "is like rain falling from the sky into a river or pool. There is nothing but water. It's impossible to divide the sky-water from the land-water. When a little stream enters the sea, who could separate its waters back out again? Think of a bright light pouring into a room from two large windows: it enters from different places but becomes one light. Maybe this is what St. Paul meant when he said, 'Whoever is joined to God becomes one spirit with him.'"[16]

We may try to clothe with words and images this receptive depth, in which giving and receiving circulate as one, but ultimately the silence of awareness sheds them all. As light and space serve as the only clothing of *David*'s luminous intelligence, so awareness is the radiance of the Light of Christ, the healing hem of His garment (Lk 8:43–48) that brings us to the deeper communion of a more radical surrender to Jesus' first resurrection command to Mary Magdalene: "Do not touch me" (Jn 20:17). For how do we grasp or capture in our sights what is already shining through our own eyes?

"Take nothing for the journey" (Mk 6:8). The implications of these words dawn on us gradually, first as torchlight, then as moonlight, and lastly as sunlight. Due to the filter of experience this journey presents itself as a movement from relative obscurity to increasing light, and so in reality it seems. Yet let us remember St. Teresa's insistence that the radiance of the sun is already risen and shining within us: "This fountainhead that shines like the sun from the center of the soul never loses its radiance. It is ever-present within the soul and nothing can diminish its beauty."[17] Why then do we have such a convincing sense of living in obscurity? Because the "wild beasts," she says, of our wild thoughts make the soul "close her eyes to everything but them."[18]

SEEING BY TORCHLIGHT

Awareness is not like a solid tabletop or flat-screen TV. Saint Diadochos says awareness is more like the sea, which, when calm, we can see right into: "When the sea is calm, fishermen can scan its depths and therefore hardly any creature moving in the water escapes their notice. But when the sea is disturbed by the winds it hides beneath its turbid and agitated waves what it was happy to reveal when it was smiling and calm; and then the fishermen's skill and cunning prove vain. The same thing happens with the contemplative power of the intellect."[19] The ocean depth of awareness can be gazed into. This is the invitation of interior silence. We look right into the mind, right into awareness itself in which thoughts and feelings appear and disappear, whether they are like troubled, stormy waters or feathery ocean foam.

Saint Hesychios says the practice of watchful awareness yields "continuous insight into the heart's depths, stillness of mind unbroken even by thoughts which appear to be good, and the capacity to be empty of all thought."[20] The deeper our insight into these depths, "the greater the longing with which you will pray."[21] Saint Teresa also knows this depth-dimension of awareness: "I used to be tormented by this turmoil of thoughts," she recalls. "A little over four years ago I came to realize by experience that thinking is not the same as mindfulness.... I hadn't been able to understand why, if the mind is one of the faculties of the soul, it is sometimes so restless. Thoughts fly around so fast.... It was driving me crazy to see the faculties of my soul calmly absorbed in the remembrance of God while my thoughts, on the other hand were wildly agitated."[22] She learns from her own experience that there is something deep within her that remains absorbed in prayer even amid the whirl of thoughts in her head.

Saint Hesychios sees a direct link between our growth in watchful awareness and the gradual manifestation of the Light of Christ. The two are simultaneous: the more stable and expansive our awareness, the greater the suffusion of awareness in Light. This gradual realization of the loving light of awareness is the simplest and most profound thing that can happen in our lives this side of death. It reveals death's double-hinged doors.

Whatever blessings we may receive in our devotional lives, our family lives, our lives spent in service of God and neighbor, our contemplative lives will keep us very practically focused for quite some time on the ordeal of our thoughts. This ordeal of thoughts is the making of the contemplative. Whether feelings of being blessed or consoled are absent or abundant, cultivating the practice of vigilant awareness is vital.

In an early season of practice we are so caught up in our thoughts and feelings that we think we are these thoughts and feelings and miss the distinction between thoughts and awareness that St. Teresa and countless others have discovered.

The great masters presume this awkwardness we all know and so they teach in a practical way the cultivation of awareness.

When the light of awareness illumines no more than a torch does, we should expect innumerable variations of a couple of interior movements. By far the most common experience is to find ourselves forever chasing thoughts. Saint Hesychios observes, "As soon as a thought appears in our minds we chase after it and become embroiled in it."[23] When we become embroiled in our thoughts, we immediately become one of the cast of characters in the inner drama. Often the lines of this scripted interiority are something like "Oh my goodness, I've become embroiled in my thoughts," or "I shouldn't be having any thoughts," or "I'm so bad at this." Often this script is accompanied by a demented stage director, who stays out of sight but is always within our range of hearing: "blame others without relent"; "envy others' success"; "compare yourself with others to enflame your own self-loathing"; "victimize others to avoid your own pain." These inner commentaries do nothing but embroil us more deeply and add to a lifetime's momentum of deriving our sense of self from whatever it is in us that talks and talks and talks and talks and talks to ourselves about all this.

As an antidote St. Hesychios offers a simple practice of awareness: "closely scrutinize every mental image or provocation."[24] His suggestion is deceptively simple. Normally we are so caught up in the mind-stream of our thoughts that before we know it, we are swept along. In order to practice what St. Hesychios is teaching we have to stop chasing the thoughts, if only for a moment. We usually find that we cannot do this very well. But with practice of this inner turning around, however, and stopping long enough to look squarely at these thoughts, we learn that we can do this. In this way we do exactly what Jesus did during the temptation in the desert (Mt 4:1–11). He refused to get caught up in inner commentary. Instead he recited short passages of Scripture.[25] When St. Hesychios says that awareness consists in closely scrutinizing thoughts, he is trying to place us in a different relationship with the thoughts. He is not telling us that thoughts should not be there if they happen to be there. Putting his advice into practice will, over (much) time, help us learn to be an engaged and receptively detached witness of all this inner commentary that appears and disappears in our mind. Gradually we learn to stop deriving our sense of identity from this habitual inner chatter no matter how incessantly it continues to chatter.

Evagrius insists as strongly as St. Hesychios on the importance of cultivating this first stage of watchful awareness. In our discovery of inner stillness, we first learn a good deal more about our obsessive mental habits than about inner stillness. But Evagrius is convinced that this ordeal with thoughts is crucial to our contemplative training and that we should take every opportunity to observe all we can about these thoughts; which thoughts "are less frequent in their assaults, which are more distressing, which yield the field more readily and which are the more resistant."[26] He is not trying to get us to have no afflictive thoughts (this would halt our contemplative training) but to stop, turn around, and look right into them. "Observe their intensity," he says, "their periods of decline and follow them as they rise and fall."[27] Note whether there is anger by itself or anger and fear. How long does it last? What sets it off? "What is the order of their succession and the nature of their associations."[28] In order to "observe their intensity," their "rise and fall," or the "order of their succession," we have to withdraw our attention from the inner commentaries, be still before them, and eventually look right into them, right through them. Even if they continue their chatter for another decade or so, we simply remain before them "profoundly silent and still and in praying."[29] Thus we gradually move from agitated victim to silent witness.

This simple, sifting, spiritual skill of watchful awareness changes our relationship with any sort of thought or feeling. Normally we are caught up in the story we tell ourselves about the thought or feeling. Say, for example, we become easily envious of people who wear expensive clothes, "Look what she's wearing! Who does she think she is with that Chanel jacket and that ridiculous Louis Vuitton bag. Typical of her. Absolutely typical. She'd be better off with a tongue stud." The story threads along, and we miss the simple envy that set it off. Or perhaps we are so easily threatened because we compensate for our sense of inadequacy through expensive clothing and as a result are stitched right into the weave of this inner chatter.

The variety of these dramas is endless. What is important is that we can observe as much as possible, but not in order to replace it with another drama, such as "I shouldn't be this way" or "I shouldn't be having these thoughts." The practice of awareness gradually enables us to meet whatever happens, before we begin to talk to ourselves about what has happened. Over time, things change. We experience simple fear, anger, shame, calm, joy, pride instead of an inner commentary on the fear, anger, shame, calm, joy, pride. It is the inner chatter that keeps us enslaved.

What are the effects of the practice of awareness at this early phase of seeing only by torchlight? We grow in the ability to turn around and see our thoughts and feelings (no matter what their strength) as simple events distinct from the tempest of stories we relate to ourselves (and likely to others) about them. Whatever it is in us that grasps and craves is soothed and calmed and begins to loosen its grip. The inner chatter needs this craving in order to cling. But inner chatter cannot cling to simple awareness. It simply appears and disappears in awareness like so much weather moving through the valley. Thoughts slow down, we feel more spacious within. That which sees the thought arise and fall is free of it and free to pray in the midst of it. This is what St. Teresa discovered for herself, and so can we.

This is the first phase of the expansion of awareness, a phase we return to over and again as needed: learning to scrutinize, learning to observe without commenting on what is happening within us instead of being dragged back into the inner chatter that serves as cloth for the fashionable outfit of a new identity. The clothing of alienation requires no emperor.

With this sense of inner spaciousness, we are less reactive to and more receptive of all manner of inner movements. This spaciousness is inherently still, poised, and watchful. Watchful inner stillness does not mean the absence of struggle, but stillness in the midst of struggle, "profoundly still and in praying."[30]

MOONRISE IN THE HEART

"A donkey going round and round in a mill cannot step out of the circle to which it is tethered."[31] This is how St. Hesychios describes the state of awareness that is held prisoner to inner chatter. Although we may feel perfectly at home with going around and around and around in circles of inner chatter, he says that this actually blinds us to something deeper: "with our inner eye blinded, we cannot perceive holiness or the radiant light of Jesus."[32] But with sufficient cultivation of watchfulness, our attention can be liberated from this mill, if only for brief periods. We begin to move from a sense of our interior life as narrow, flat, cramped, and tethered, to a real sense of inner spaciousness that is neither asinine nor tethered to anything at all.

The donkeys of our dull obsessions may be walking around and around the mill, but the ground on which they tread, the ground of their monotonous bondage, is solid and still, extending for miles and miles into open countryside.

When we glimpse something of this wide-open space within (despite the fact that our donkeys remain), we have begun to awaken to the depths of the present moment simply because we have a changed relationship with the clouds of dust kicked up by our inner chatter.

We discover something of what St. Diadochos meant when he likened our awareness to the sea that we can look right into and "scan its depths" when the waves on the surface of awareness have calmed.[33] This marks an important transition. Saint Hesychios described an earlier state of awareness in which we simply observed our thoughts under the torchlight of Christ carried in the hand of the intellect "along the tracks of the mind."[34] Note, however, that Christ is not considered to be an object of awareness, but the reason why awareness is becoming more luminous. Aided by the light of the torch that we grasped firmly, we had a good deal of work to do: battling with thoughts, scrutinizing thoughts, cultivating watchfulness. But now St. Hesychios says this luminous dimension of awareness has nothing more to do with grasping a torch. "Now the Light of awareness appears to us like a full moon, circling the heart's firmament."[35] We cannot grasp moonlight even as we are bathed in it. Walking by torchlight along the tracks of the mind has now led us to the threshold of our Center, a Center that is everywhere, what the ancients called "the heart."[36] For some this is a gradual transition, for others a decisive breakthrough.

It really does not matter; for in either case there are several characteristics of this inner expansion of the heart.

THE PULL OF THE MOON

The creative momentum of returning to our practice whenever we become aware that our attention has been stolen is now completely well established. This itself implies that there has been an expansion of awareness. We spend less time battling with the fact that there are thoughts stealing our attention. We have more or less stopped commenting to ourselves on the fact that we are forever commenting on the incessant commentaries in our heads. We let the mind be, just as we let the weather be. Whereas before we simply believed we were this constantly changing weather—now storm, now sun, now deluge, now drought, now week after week of grim gray weather—the realization is dawning on us that we are not this ever-changing weather of inner commentary.

There is an abiding, and increasingly stable, inner calm and spaciousness that allows us to behold our life circumstances with greater ease and wider perspective. It is as though, at the earlier stage, we had encountered our inner battles as we would encounter a bee inside a telephone booth. The same bees are experienced very differently now that we know ourselves not as narrow and tight, but as wide-open and endless fields, where the soul can "bathe in its own space," as David Scott puts it, and "make long swathes in meadow lengths of space."[37] This is what Evagrius calls that "open country whose name is prayer."[38]

If our practice has featured the use of a prayer word, it is common not to have to repeat it consciously (though we are completely free to). There is a practical, fundamental unity between the concentration of attention (facilitated by the prayer word) and the expansion of awareness. The two are as one. It is impossible to separate the concentrated plop of a pebble in a pond from the water's widening ripples of reception. With this expansion of awareness comes an inner stability in the midst of the joys, ordeals, or tedium of daily life however it happens to be.

The present moment has an utterly reliable way of being exactly the way it is at any given moment. This paradox of the inner unity of concentrated expansion has opened up the present moment, revealing in this "sunlit absence" life as firm and unshakable as it is an ungraspable flow: unshakable because it is our foundation; ungraspable, because it is constantly being poured out as sheer gift. This inner stability is the fruit of a maturing practice of contemplation: "Continuity of attention produces inner stability; inner stability produces a natural intensification of watchfulness and in due measure gives contemplative insight into spiritual warfare. This in turn is succeeded by persistence in the Jesus

Prayer . . . in which the mind, free from all images, enjoys complete silence."[39]

The rising of the moon exerts a powerful pull on the earth and its waters. Likewise the moonrise of Christ's presence in the heart's sky exerts a powerful draw on our awareness. This is different from seeing by torchlight. Seeing by torchlight focuses on cultivating skills of watchfulness with respect to what appears in awareness. Seeing by moonlight is not an increase in the things we need to be aware of, but the expansive opening up of awareness from within. Awareness opens and expands in response to the pull of the rising moon of Presence in the sky of the heart. However, with this moonrise come new challenges as well; for it is very easy to get caught in the allure of the moon.

THE ALLURE OF THE MOON

After we have been long dedicated to silent prayer and experience it largely as restful and peaceful, it is easy enough to feel quite happy simply to stretch out in this hammock of contemplative practice and enjoy a martini of quietude. In this case we have managed to avoid the pull of the moon on our awareness and instead have become besotted by the moon's allure.

This is not to deny the real progress we have made over the years in prayer and service. Guided by torchlight we have learned to step carefully along the road, negotiating inner battles. There has been unquestionable development in the accuracy of our self-knowledge; we know the crucial distinction between any sort of interior weather and the mountain on which this weather comes and goes. We probably have experienced (perhaps even for long periods) an undeniable inner recollection. But this new challenge is typically that of the seasoned intermediate.

Just because our practice has led us to a certain inner calm and recollection, we should not assume that we are home and free. Saint Augustine speaks to this when he says, "Take care that a time of calm repose does not lead to laxity and forgetfulness of God."[40] There is a way to recognize the state of awareness that indicates when this calm repose has been besotted by the allure of the moon. Very soon after settling into our practice (if not immediately after), a dull, inattentive, graying-out settles in. There may be the entire spectrum of thoughts flowing by, but, while we are not quite caught up in reacting to them, we are more or less immersed in them and being swept along passively with them. Yet we feel fairly restful and content with it all. These thoughts don't have the blaring narrative of the previous season. By contrast these thoughts are thick and dense, characterized by a lethargic calm that is really a dulling of awareness. This dulling of awareness is not terribly far from a state of dozing off. In fact it is not uncommon for the occasional snore to serve as our reminder to return to our practice. But often we do not fall quite asleep and, while we are certainly not alert, we find we can pray for an hour or more resting in this comfy hammock and its martini of mantra. If someone looked at us sitting in prayer, he or she would not see an engaged and vigilant peace in our face and bearing, but instead a drooping face ready to nod off at any moment; the breath is short and shallow, as far from the abdomen as possible; the body not alert but slightly hunched over. Admittedly this hammock of prayer is rather comfy. But it is not enough to stay in this nice place. We do well to cooperate actively and work with our attention, with the support of our own body and breath.

The contemplative's inner stance is not one of being swept downriver along with everything else. The contemplative's repose is not a passive state but an engaged, silent receptivity, "an ever moving repose," as St. Maximus the Confessor calls it.[41] Like a riverbed, which is constantly receiving and letting go in the very same moment. Vigilant receptivity and nonclinging release are one and the same for this riverbed awareness as it constantly receives all coming from upstream while at the very same moment releasing all downstream. The receptive letting-go of this riverbed stillness characterizes what the pull of the moon "rising in the firmament heart" is trying to teach us.

Saint Isaac the Syrian teaches us to "Love silence above all things, because it brings you near to the fruit that the tongue cannot express . . .and, then, from out of this silence something is born that leads to silence itself."[42] If we stay in the comfy hammock of lethargic inattentiveness, we slow our cooperation with what is trying to come to birth.

Awareness is born from the silence that draws us and "leads to Silence itself." Awareness is another name for Silence itself.

As we work with our attention in our practice, it often seems as though we are excavating a mountain with a spoon. But we gradually sense that we are encountering something deeper. The prayer word flows directly into an ocean depth of awareness, deeper than the reach of the senses. Saint Hesychios says of watchful awareness: "Its branches reach to the seas and to deep abysses of contemplation, its shoots to the rivers of the beauteous and divine mysteries."[43] When we plumb the depths of our practice we are embraced by a Living Presence that has known us from all eternity (Jer 1:5). In this knowing Presence in which Knower and known are as one, the prayer word and the flowing vastness of simple awareness are one. Presuming the Jesus Prayer as one's prayer word, Saint Hesychios says we can look right into the mind: "The more closely attentive you are to your mind, the greater the longing with which you pray to Jesus. . . . Just as close attentiveness brilliantly illumines the mind, so the lapse from watchfulness and from the sweet invocation of Jesus will darken it completely."[44] This brilliant illumination that St. Hesychios refers to is always present within us, shining like the sun (cloud cover or not); though this fact of perpetual presence only gradually dawns on our everyday mind first "in the intellect like a torch," then more deeply and expansively in the "heart's firmament," and now in the innermost depths of the heart "like the sun."[45]

SUNRISE IN THE HEART

Saint Teresa of Avila goes to great lengths to remind us that there is such a thing as inner light. "We are conditioned," she says, "to perceive only external light. We forget that there is such a thing as inner light, illuminating our soul, and we mistake that radiance for darkness."[46] Saint Hesychios says our practice will dawn with yet a new brilliance, a "continuous seeing into the heart's depths, stillness of mind unbroken even by thoughts which appear to be good and the capacity to be empty of thoughts."[47] With the training in silent prayer that we have learnt by torchlight and then by moonlight, our inner gaze is stilled and steadied in such a way that this inner light begins to dawn as brightly as the sun: "Just as those who look at the sun cannot but fill their eyes with light, so they who always have a steady gaze into their heart cannot fail to be illumined."[48] This discovery was one of St. Augustine's great realizations; he sees that this inner light is itself illumined by Light shining in light: "the very light that shone in my eyes was mine no longer. For the light was within."[49] For Augustine and for many of the saints and sages, this is a glimpse of what the Psalmist glimpsed, "In your light, Lord, we see light" (Ps 36:10). This is the liberating, rich poverty of contemplation: our practice is reduced to the sheer simplicity of Light shining in light. This is what *David* bodies forth in his Florentine gallery of light.

The luminous simplicity of this grounding awareness is beyond the reach of doubt. Saint Diadochos understates his solid surety of this when he says: "You should not doubt that the intellect, when it begins to be strongly energized by the divine light, becomes so completely translucent that it sees its own light vividly."[50] When certain inner conditions are ready and ripe, the ground of awareness opens up from within; the sun dawns, and we are utterly free of shackles. Our life circumstances, however, whether grim or glad, remain with us. Our character's quirks remain firmly in place. But we are free in the midst of both sorrow and joy; free and gracious enough to welcome and respond to the present moment however it happens to be. We cannot pull this off ourselves, because what we usually take to be this "self" that likes to accomplish such spiritual feats as "awakening" or "enlightenment" has fallen away, lost (Mt 16:25), if only momentarily, like a crystal in sunlight.

Something "ever ancient ever new"[51] dawns in awareness, not as an object of awareness, for it is too close to us for that, but as "a sunlit absence,"[52] interior to awareness itself, "more intimate to me than my inmost self" as St. Augustine famously phrased it.[53]

To the conceptual mind this awakening differs from previous ones. This luminous, flowing Vastness is constantly present whether we turn our gaze within or without, for in this Vastness there is no within versus without. This ground-awareness does not joust with divine presence-versus-absence, for it embraces both. It is beyond any possibility of doubt, for awareness saturates both doubt and consent, and its silence embraces both fear and trust. It is as Teflon to both past and future. Untouched by time, but without being excluded by time, it is yet within time but without being contained by time.[54] Too simple to come and go, it is the "fullness of time" (Gal 4:4).

When we look within, the "I" that looks is saturated by this Vastness; when we look without, this "I" is liberated of itself by its immersion in the very Vastness that indwells it (Jn 14:10; 17:22–23), much like the sponge that is immersed in the ocean depth that fills its every membrane. When the sponge looks out, it sees only ocean; when it looks within, it sees only ocean. We are graciously immersed in Jesus' own awareness of the simplest of facts: "He who sees me sees the Father" (Jn 14:7). "The Father and I are one" (Jn 12:45). To lose our life

(Mt 10:39) is to find it "hidden with Christ in God" (Col 3:3), in the overflowing, simple suchness of what is.

Not only is this blossoming of awareness from within a depthless depth out of reach of doubt's arthritic grip but also it presents itself as always having been present throughout our entire personal history. It quite rightly seems to us that there has been a slow, gradual blossoming, but once this blossom has opened it is obvious that the depthless depth of awareness has always been this open, sunlit absence. This realization is just another roadside paradox of the spiritual path. This absence is not the lack of something that ought to be there, but the overflowing of Vastness as right *Now*. The inner Vastness that overflows as *Now*, in which all of us "live and move and have our being" (Acts 17:28), cannot be absent, not due to any constraint, but due to the naked simplicity of its freedom. Certainly this spacious, silent land can seem to be absent or distant to the distracted, discursive, calculating, or frenzied mind. But to the still mind of the inner eye, "the eye of the heart,"[55] or the "gaze of the mind,"[56] as Augustine calls it, it is and always has been closer to us than we are to ourselves.

The sun of awareness in the gaze of the heart is not a heightened state of awareness that soon descends into a trough of awareness only again to ascend the heights. The Vastness of awareness itself grounds all these changing states of mind. The condensation of our innumerable states of mind—thoughts, mood, and character—is an ever-changing pattern of weather. But this terrain of mountains and valleys of simple awareness witnesses all these changing patterns of weather as they move through our psychological terrain, changing as all weather changes. The heart's vastness receives pain, strife, confusion, fear, anger, frenzy, yet is untouched by pain, strife, confusion, fear, anger, frenzy. It is as immediately present to pain or illness that is being healed as it is to pain or illness that is not being healed. It receives and lets go as a riverbed receives and lets go—both at the same instant—of all the water of daily life the river carries along.

Awareness itself, the very *aware-ing*, is never awareness of some *thing*, yet by virtue of its simplicity it grounds all things and therefore is never separate from anything. The gaze of the heart is always gazing into God, for this is quite simply what the heart's depth does. R. S. Thomas states more clearly the inherent paradox of gazing into God:

Because it is not I who look
but I who am looked through, Gloria.[57]

This undeniable luminous Vastness that slips out of any clothing that mere words can weave, but of which every tongue must tell, is not a physical light that occurs in space and time. Saints and sages throughout the tradition frequently warn us about thinking of it as a physical form. Saint Augustine reminds us that, while he was busy concerning himself "only with things that are contained in space, this light was not in space."[58] Evagrius says the demon "cunningly manipulates the brain and converts the light surrounding the intellect into a form."[59] Saint Diadochos warns that if this light "has a shape [it] is the product of the evil artifice of the enemy."[60] He insists that we should not take up a spiritual path "in hope of seeing visions clothed with form or shape; for if we do Satan will find it easy to lead our soul astray. Our one point is to perceive the love of God fully and consciously in our heart."[61]

Why the insistence that this inner light has no shape? Academic theology reminds us that this mystery we call God is beyond what can be grasped as shape and form in the way we grasp tangible things. Saint Teresa gets straight to the point when she says it is because "It is all about love melting in love."[62] Saint John of the Cross would suggest that this is not a blurring of identities but just the way things are. "It seems to such a person that the entire universe is a sea of love in which it is engulfed, for conscious of the living point or center of love within itself, it is unable to catch a sight of the boundaries of love."[63] This realization is not a confusion of the discursive mind's conceptual distinction of Creator from creature but creation's ultimate clarity and consummation.

On the spiritual path "we walk by faith and not by sight" (2 Cor 5:7). The full splendor of the sun of awareness reveals the most ordinary daily events to be transparent to *David*'s splendid gallery of light. This is the Fact: our liberating reduction to porous simplicity: the infinitely luminous expanse of right Now. "This light itself is one, and all those are one who see it and love it."[64]

FIVE

Sifted by Boredom

Like thirsty ground I yearn for you.
Quick, Yahweh, answer me before my
spirit fails.
>   —Psalm 143:6–8.

My body pines for you like a
Dry, weary land without water.
>   —Psalm 63:2

The abbess of Crewe apparently found prayer boring. Muriel Spark's novel *The Abbess of Crewe* has as its main character a larger-than-life monastic superior with not only expensive tastes but also a curious idiosyncrasy with respect to her prayer. While gathered together with the entire community for their regular praying of the psalms in Latin, the abbess instead recites to herself lines of English poetry. Indeed there is much nourishment provided by poetry. Nevertheless, the question arises: What was going on within the abbess of Crewe that the psalms ceased to provide her the spiritual nourishment she presumably once enjoyed? Was the daily round of prayer becoming boring? Muriel Spark does not pursue this question in her delightful novel of political intrigue and vote rigging. But the question nevertheless highlights something of great importance on the spiritual path.

What do we do when a way of praying that had once been satisfying, nourishing, and fervent is now experienced as dry, boring, futile, and paralytically unsatisfying? This is no easy matter. No matter what our walk in life, if prayer is the integrating component of our life, this can hit rather hard and make us think we have lost our prayer life or even our way in life. Whatever the case may be, there are important times in the life of prayer when all the juice seems to run out, and our prayer life seems to have evaporated. This often sets us searching for some other form of prayer that will provide more juice, a greater buzz—anything to help keep this transitional boredom at bay.

Many, indeed very many, stop praying altogether when met by this brick wall of boredom. The abbess of Crewe simply coped as best she could. But if her prayer life, or anybody's for that matter, was going to deepen, becoming bored with forms of prayer that involve a lot of words and mental effort, or even dogged by a sense of prayer's biting futility, is a commonly occurring sign that prayer is deepening by means of a sort of creative disintegration. Like compost, prayer breaks down into fertile matter for the life around it. Prayer matures by a process of breaking down rather than by acquisition and spiritual prowess. This simplification can for a time (perhaps quite some time) feel as though we are going backward, or worse, going no place at all.

Why should this happen? Why should boredom beset prayer? What's wrong with a buzzing, caffeinated fervor day in and day out? The reason for this aridity is not that prayer is suddenly dying. Aridity sets in for more or less lengthy and difficult periods when our prayer life is deepening and the nature and dynamic of prayer is beginning to change.

Our five senses, along with the discursive (or thinking) mind, deal with objects (whether conceptual or physical objects) and are predisposed to and preoccupied with feeling, thinking, perceiving, language, stimulation, and feedback. But God is not an object in the way these things are objects. God cannot be grasped the way other things are grasped by our normal ways of knowing and perceiving. For us to move deeply into God's deep movement in us, "whose margins are God's margins," as R. S. Thomas puts it, the senses must learn to abide in stillness.[1] But because we are accustomed to so much stimulation, our initial encounters with deeper levels of stillness tend to register as boredom or deprivation of something that we think should be there. With time and perseverance this stillness will register differently, not as boredom, but as a free-flowing vastness and liberating peace that has no opposite, and so embraces all opposites, both boredom and zeal. In this silent land we are taught gradually to "walk by faith and not by sight" (2 Cor 5:7).

In his *Confessions* St. Augustine comments on the significance of Christ's resurrection and ascension: Christ "has gone from our sight so that we should 'return to our heart' (Is 46:8) and find him there."[2] The heart, a term that refers not to our thoughts and feelings but to our innermost depths that ground thought and feeling, our knowing center, is the place of divine encounter. Just because the Risen Christ is not accessible to the senses in the way the historical Jesus was, this does not imply absence but draws us to a Presence that is deeper than our discursive and imagining powers can perceive, but in which the heart delights. For here, Augustine insists, "God speaks in the great silence of the heart."[3] When boredom besets prayer that is built on firm foundations of love of God and neighbor, boredom is a sign that the senses are being led from trying to grasp God as an object to a deep stillness that receives rather than grasps.

Several things come to the fore as prayer deepens. Prayer becomes less and less something that we do and think about and more a matter of *just being* (the phrase starts to make practical sense). As the anonymous author of the *Book of Privy Counselling* says, "not what you are but *that* you are."[4] At the same time the role the discursive or thinking mind plays begins to change. We are being drawn more deeply into relationship with what our senses cannot grasp any more than a sponge can grasp the ocean, even though its entire membrane is saturated with ocean and seems to be as much ocean as membrane. As we move further out into the depths, other aspects of mind begin to awaken, what ancient theology calls the "flower of the mind," the "apex of the mind," the "scintilla" or "spark of the soul." The surface aspects of mind play a less dominant role and remain ever-focused on what prayer feels like, asking such things as "Am I praying well?" "Am I doing this right?" Boredom serves both to signal and to facilitate this transition, this changing of the guard.

Prayer is not content to stay up in the branches of our minds with all the other things we think about; it works its way down through the branches and trunk, into our roots where it is one with the Ground of all. We gradually (and at times with reluctance) learn to be a servant of this process not so much by letting go of thoughts (which often won't let go of us) but by releasing more deeply into our practice. But thoughts, too, point to, emerge from, and manifest this Ground. Our very being doesn't have to pray. We are already prayer.

SIFTED BY BOREDOM

From early adulthood Margaret felt strongly drawn to prayer and service. She found employment teaching adults how to read and said her prayer life also "really began to take off at this time." She had been raised in a Christian denomination and normally attended its weekly services.

She felt strongly committed to this, but what really began to draw her, and this she had never experienced before, was to spend some time each day praying on her own. She found that she could reclaim part of the morning by getting up an hour or so before the rest of her family. Her prayer featured saying certain prayers that she had known since childhood and praying for other people's needs, which she really felt moved to do. Another feature was reading the Bible, especially the Gospels.

She said the Scriptures simply came alive for her. "Every scene, every character, every deed or saying of Jesus was as engaging and vivid as anything I could watch on TV. But I was also in those scenes." She felt constantly nourished and sustained during this time of prayer. She cast her net deeply into the Gospels (Lk 5:4). There were also periods during the day when she could turn to prayer, and often during her lunch break at work she would visit a quiet church or park nearby, where she would pray for fifteen or twenty minutes. Apart from occasional exceptions, these times of prayer were a fixture in her life. But for no apparent reason her experience of prayer began to change.

What had previously provided spiritual nourishment and a clear sense of God's presence in her life was now becoming grindingly tedious. Her morning practice of praying with Scripture became laborious and fidgety. What had buoyed her up was now burdensome. Prayers of thanksgiving and intercession seemed to be halfhearted. She didn't really want to say these prayers. She didn't want to *say* any prayers and yet she didn't feel ungrateful to God or indifferent to the needs of the many people who asked to be remembered in prayer. This began to upset her. What had been light, peace, and dedication was now dull, dark, and patchy. She thought she was losing her prayer life.

She continued to get up in the morning to pray, but the most she could do was sit in her chair with her Bible merely open. Her prayer was highly distracted, whereas before it was engaged and focused. This became the new norm.

She wrestled with this collapse in her prayer life for some time before she realized that she actually preferred simply to sit there, just be there. Over time her way of praying changed from prayer that involved a lot of mental activity (reading, reflecting, giving thanks, interceding, etc.) to simply being still in the presence of God, tinged with the feeling that she was not very good at prayer. While she felt guilty about this "sitting there doing nothing," as she put it, she admitted being aware of a strong attraction to do just that. "Just sit there and *be*." Still she felt, however, that this couldn't possibly be right, so she learned about other styles of praying with the hope that the sense of prayer as futile boredom would go away. But these new prayer strategies did not last long. She soon found them likewise laborious. And so she just sat still because it was the only thing she could do if she was going to pray.

What Margaret experienced is actually quite a common pattern and she was surprised to learn that one of the great spiritual masters of the Christian tradition, St. John of the Cross, had described much of what she was going through.

When our prayer life begins to be reduced to the simplicity of contemplation, one of the first things to happen is that we find we cannot pray in the manner that we have been drawn to and grown accustomed to. Saint John of the Cross identifies three signs that indicate that a person's prayer life is beginning to simplify into contemplation: "The first sign is the realization that one cannot make discursive meditation or receive satisfaction from it as before. Dryness is now the outcome of fixing the senses on subjects that formerly provided satisfaction."[5] By "discursive meditation," he means any form of prayer that involves a good deal of mental activity, reflection, devotion, imagining Bible scenes, saying set prayers—all the work of the thinking mind. Earlier these forms of prayer contributed crucially to forging a strong relationship with God and building good habits of regular prayer, but whereas they previously buoyed us up, they now begin to weigh us down.

This should not strike us as esoteric. Any gardener knows how important it is to get watering right with new plants. If you water them too much, they may look just fine, but due to the frequent watering, the roots do not develop properly because they have not had to dig deeply in search of water, since it's all being supplied on the surface. This is why after a sufficient amount of watering early on, the gardener lets up on the watering. The subsequent dryness makes the plant put down roots deeper into the soil in search of a more consistent though less abundant source. This strengthens the plant against disease and drought.

Saint John of the Cross sees this inability to pray as a sign of growth. After we "have been fed somewhat and have become in a certain fashion accustomed to spiritual things and acquired some fortitude and constancy, God begins to wean the soul, as they say, and place it in a state of contemplation."[6] As John sees it, this inability to pray as we previously did is a natural response to the nourishment prayer is providing.

A second sign that prayer is developing is that not only are we unable to pray in the discursive manner we once did, but we feel *disinclined* to pray in the way we once did. We become aware, he says, "of a disinclination to fix the imagination or sense faculties on other particular objects, exterior or interior."[7] John of the Cross is not suggesting that just because we are having a bad prayer day and don't feel like praying that this is somehow a sign of growth. He is presuming that our prayer, like Margaret's, is marked by dedication and consistency. This disinclination to pray is not laziness but something that befalls consistent, dedicated prayer as a sign of maturing simplification.

The third sign and "the surest," according to John, "is that the person likes to remain alone in loving awareness of

God," instead of practicing the devotions and praying with words that previously characterized prayer.[8] The attraction to solitude and movement into solitude is the outstanding feature of Jesus' own prayer life. In the Gospels, Jesus is routinely going off to some deserted place in order to commune with the Father (Lk 5:13). This solitude is quite the opposite of isolation. In fact it has no more to do with wanting to be alone than the desire to climb to the top of the mountain is a reaction to being tired of the plains. People head for the mountains not out of rejection of the plains, but because of the attraction of the mountains themselves.

In the Christian tradition, the authentic attraction to solitude is understood as a call, a way of responding to the attraction to God. While some people experience this more strongly than others, it is always profoundly ecclesial, that is, rooted in the community of those who genuinely seek God. The call to solitude is not a call to be alone but to *be with* God, and solitary communion with God is at the same time a solidarity with all creation. One outstanding example of this ecclesial solitude is seen in St. Anthony the Great, the so-called father of monks. He becomes aware of a profound attraction to solitude as a response to hearing the Gospel read out in church.[9] Dietrich Bonhoeffer has perhaps the most succinct way of expressing this intrinsic harmony of solitude and community: "Whoever cannot be alone should beware of community. Whoever cannot stand being in community should beware of being alone."[10]

Solitude is a response to and an expression of a vital sense of solidarity with all people. This is quite different from merely being alone because we cannot abide other people or meet life on its own terms. God knows we know what that is like, but it is not solitude, the Christlike sign that our prayer is beginning to excavate the Kingdom of the present moment and widen our capacity for compassion. Nor does St. John of the Cross think this attraction to solitude is reserved to friars and nuns. *The Living Flame of Love*, in which he describes these characteristics, was written for a laywoman, Ana de Penalosa. We don't know a great deal about the development of her prayer life. Perhaps she experienced something of what Margaret experienced.

Feeling boxed in by her own struggles, Margaret could only gradually see that the apparent collapse of her prayer life as she knew it was a sign of transition. But to any listener skilled in the practice of contemplation, Margaret showed all the classic signs of this creative disintegration. After a formative period of generous dedication to saying prayers and using scenes from Scripture as vehicles of reverent prayer, she started to become not only disinclined but also unable to do so. She actually preferred simply to sit alone in silent prayer, lovingly attentive to God, whose obscurity was slowly becoming the vehicle of an intimate presence too near to be felt. "Prayer has become a simple resting in a presence I cannot feel yet somehow know. I don't feel I've made any progress in prayer. It's more like everything about my prayer life has been taken away and this resting in God is the only thing left. I'm not sure why I call it 'resting in God,' but those words seem to fit. It usually feels as though I'm wasting my time."

Margaret has never so much as heard of St. John of the Cross (and, frankly, there would be a lot about him that she wouldn't like), yet she is nearly paraphrasing him. He says it is important for "the soul to remain in rest and quietude even though it may seem obvious to them that they are doing nothing and wasting time, and even though they think this disinclination to think about anything is due to their laxity. Through patience and perseverance in prayer, they will be doing a great deal without activity on their part."[11] He is consistent in his advice to let go of "the impediment and fatigue of ideas and thoughts, and care not about thinking and discursive meditation."[12] Saint John of the Cross knows how strong the tendency may be to force oneself back into those ways of praying that involve a lot of mental activity, even though we now find this heavy baggage to carry.

This pressure can also be imposed on us by people who know little about the simplifying dynamics of contemplation and tell us to stay with a former way of praying, which has now become too burdensome, in spite of our longing, however obscure, simply to be silent. Saint John of the Cross says this "is like hammering the horseshoe instead of the nail."[13] This is an effective simile, for it expresses how a single act produces a twofold error: "on the one hand they do harm, and on the other hand they receive no profit."[14]

When the prayerful narratives that go on in our heads first begin to be enfolded into silence, it will register as boredom to that aspect of our minds that talks and talks and talks. This was Margaret's case. Her boredom with her heady, discursive way of praying, her subsequent disinclination and inability to pray in her former manner took her by the hand and led her by means of loss and poverty to simply being.

In contrast to Margaret, there are many people who feel drawn from the very beginning to a manner of praying that is already contemplative in its orientation. They don't escape this trial either. This was Benjamin's experience of praying the Jesus Prayer, but his case is not as fruitful as Margaret's.

DERAILED BY BOREDOM

Benjamin had always felt a strong attraction to silent prayer. Other forms of prayer did not satisfy the yearning he had just to be silent. After some instruction in the practice of contemplation, Benjamin gave himself generously to this way of prayer that he said felt "so natural and simple." He found a shortened form of the Jesus Prayer to be very useful for providing his mind with something to focus on. "I found the line by St. John Climacus 'Let the name of Jesus cling to your breath, and you will know the meaning of stillness' to be worth more than a library full of books.[15] This is the sort of thing I've been waiting for all my life."

Benjamin was generous and consistent in his practice. He was soon beginning to taste a certain amount of inner peace. This spurred him on in his practice. But then after several weeks of dedicated practice he started experiencing boredom when he had been experiencing calm delight and refreshment. He didn't like this. So he stopped praying.

He still feels very drawn to silent prayer. But instead of practicing contemplation he instead reads everything he can get his hands on about the practice of contemplation. We may be able to get our hands on a good book about contemplation, but we cannot get our hands around contemplation itself.

Why is boredom such a testing ground? Why does it tread so predictably—at least in some degree—on the heels of the dedicated person of prayer? Boredom is really a sign that the mind is beginning to assume, as it were, a posture of release and receptivity. Our thinking mind has a strong tendency to grasp, whether it is the grasp of comprehension or the grasping frenzy of mind-tripping. The thinking dimension of the mind needs to keep a tight grip on things. But when we move into the depths of prayer this grip has a way of becoming a pounding fist in its demand to control and to understand. This fist of comprehension is gradually being softened and opened up during deep prayer, exposing a new depth of the mind, an engaged and receptive depth, that is deeper than what thinks, reacts, plots, and schemes. This depth of the mind is more like an open palm than a clenched fist. It does not grasp so much as release, receive, and let be. But because the thinking mind so dominates, there can be a bit of stiffness as it opens. This stiffness registers in the mind as boredom. With nothing for the grasping mind to do, it feels bored or even anxious.

What do we do in the presence of this boredom? Scratch our wrists. Sigh. Fidget. A story (difficult to source) is told of St. Teresa of Avila picking up her hourglass and shaking it in order to hurry it along. The saints and sages seem to know that it is important simply to sit still in the presence of boredom even if they are no good at doing it. Saint John of the Cross likens this to someone sitting for a portrait. It is important not to move. "If the model for the painting or retouching of a portrait should move because of a desire to do something else, since it cannot do anything or think of anything in prayer, the artist would be unable to finish and the work would be spoiled."[16] During this period of boredom in prayer, it is natural to try to get some sort of juice out of it, in the way of consoling feelings or inspiring insight. But it is of no use. This boredom is actually an indication that our prayer is going deeper than where our thoughts and feelings reach. Saint John of the Cross says that the more we try to prop ourselves up by thoughts and feelings "the more we will feel the lack of these, for this support cannot be supplied through these sensory means."[17] There is plenty of support from God who is the loving ground of our being, from whom nothing can separate us (Rom 8:35–39). But it is not accessible to the senses just now in the way that birdsong is or the smell of our burning supper.

If we insist on trying to wring consolation out of our rags of prayer, when God is weaning us from this consolation and leading us through the healing boredom of Israel in the desert, we will be, as John says "hammering the horseshoe instead of the nail," a waste of time that also holds us back. In fact it does feel like a great waste of time, and as a result, it is easy enough to think we are just being lazy because we are simply unable to return to an earlier way of praying that involved a good deal of thinking and reflection. Saint John of the Cross advises that despite these feelings "we should endure them peacefully."[18] And this we do "even though we think this disinclination to think about anything is due to our laxity. Through patience and perseverance in prayer, we will be doing a great deal without activity on our part."[19]

During this transitional boredom, this night of sense, we simply immerse ourselves in our practice as best we can: "Preserve a loving attentiveness to God with no desire to feel or understand any particular thing concerning God."[20]

During this sojourn in the desert, our former way of praying hinders us, and we do well simply to be; for "the considerations and meditations and acts that formerly helped the soul now hinder it, and it brings to prayer no other support than faith, hope, and love."[21] Faith, hope, and love are traditionally known as the theological virtues, the transfiguration of our memory, understanding, and will. But until all the knots have been combed out of boredom's hair, faith, hope, and love will feel for the most part like nothing at all. The way this dryness registers in the feelings will gradually change as we are integrated into the stillness that is the ground of who we are. Until then, "what we need most in order to make progress is to be silent before this great God, silent with our craving and with our tongue, for the language God best hears is the silent language of love."[22]

Perhaps in her attempt to cope with the grinding tedium of prayer, the abbess of Crewe also mulls over Samuel Taylor Coleridge's *Rime of the Ancient Mariner*. She might not be avoiding prayer at all but instead looking for support in a poem whose sentiment matches her own.

> I looked to heaven and tried to pray;
> But or ever a prayer had gusht,
> A wicked whisper came, and made
> My heart as dry as dust.[23]

She might return to the Psalms and find something similar awaiting her there: "I stretch out my hands to you, my heart like a land thirsty for you (Ps 143: 6)." Whether poet or psalmist bookend our boredom, boredom will beset us. We must learn to sit and be sifted by boredom and be accustomed to the feeling of being not very good at prayer. Prayer simplifies and deepens in no other way.

"By its very nature the mind is made to pray." So claims the fourth-century desert monk Evagrius.[24] When Evagrius says "mind" he does not mean the thinking mind (though surely we pray with our entire being).[25] He intends a deeper quality of mind than that which thinks. He means a deep, intuitive intelligence, whose especial function is to commune with God.[26] But this mind, what St. Augustine calls the "sharp point" of the mind, is like buried treasure. The special role of boredom is to sift the soil of the soul so that this treasure might emerge as silent, self-forgetful adoration. To allow this to happen we cultivate stillness. Saint John of the Cross says, "Not all of the mind's capacities have to be employed in all things, but only those that are required; as for the others, leave them unoccupied for God."[27] A farmer leaves certain fields fallow with a view to future fertility. Boredom is God's way of letting certain fields of the mind lie fallow, fields manured with boredom.

There are many types of boredom: the commuter's stretch of road, rail, or bus; the simple need for a change of pace; the tedium of cooking and eating alone; the niggling boredom of those who are strangers to themselves. And then there is always the mind-numbing preaching that pounds to a pulp an otherwise firm faith. This chapter, however, addresses only a certain type of boredom that characterizes certain periods of growth in the spiritual life.

The sense that prayer is futile, a great waste of time, that we are going nowhere, "Idle as a painted ship / Upon a painted ocean,"[28] is one of the first serious lessons in deep prayer. This lesson comes to us in different ways: to some in brief modules of a part-time course; to others as a day-in-day-out regime for which they feel ill-prepared and which can last many, many years. From our own perspective, what precisely is happening and why will likely remain hidden from us in the tangles of Providence. Yet somehow we learn to settle into it. As we till and cultivate stillness this leads not so much to yet another feeling as to the liberating insight that what *perceives*, that which is *aware* of the listless ship of boredom, is the ever-rolling, tiding Vastness of our inner depths, which are untouched by either boredom or fervor and yet are the ground of both boredom and fervor. Boredom ferries us out from the shoals of spirit into open Sea. This is the joy hidden in dry shells of prayer.

CONCLUSION

To discern that this boredom is indeed the pruning boredom of spiritual growth is the purpose of St. John of the Cross's three signs that indicate that contemplation is setting up its buds. How do we practice contemplation in the midst of this fertile boredom? As best we can, for it doesn't feel fertile. Yet we gradually grow accustomed to the feeling. One of the tasks of this aridity, which St. John of the Cross calls the night of the senses, is to help us grow accustomed to this boredom and not rely so exclusively on our feelings to gauge how prayer is going. "We walk by faith and not by sight," Paul insists (2 Cor 5: 7). This type of boredom teaches us to do just that.

It is crucial not to get caught up in the story we tell ourselves about the boredom, about how inadequate our prayer feels. John Chapman says, "We must wish to have the prayer that God gives us and no other. A distracted prayer, a desolate prayer, a happy prayer,—we must take everything as it comes."[29] On a practical level, it is important simply to return to our practice.

Spiritual boredom is an initiation into the desert and the making of any contemplative. As we journey deeper into this desert, we grow accustomed to the barrenness, and actually come to prefer it, though we might not realize this until we return to the hum of urban neon in our heads.

Boredom heals by diminishing our reliance on this spiritual glitz that keeps us preoccupied with how our prayer is progressing.

Spiritual aridity does not inhibit the normal function of our thoughts and feelings. In fact these are cleansed. As a general rule the deeper the silence, the more creative and imaginative are the interior faculties that are all grounded by this silence. And what about the role of discursive, vocal prayers, from which St. John of the Cross says we are being weaned? The key insight here is the discursive character of the prayer. Does it involve the same type of mental activity as reading, writing, or reflecting on spiritual matters or is there a deeper engagement? Boredom is part of a natural transition into simpler prayer, whatever prayer's formal shape. There is a whole range of possibility here, and each of us will discover what role discursive prayer continues to play. For some (not a few really) John Chapman's observation will seem to hit the nail on the head instead of the horseshoe when he says: "It is common enough for those who have any touch of 'Mysticism' . . . to be absolutely unable to find any meaning in vocal prayers."[30] Their path is a dry one.

Perhaps, however, St. Teresa of Avila's net catches more fish. She, too, speaks from experience, personal and pastoral, and offers a gentle yet firm rebuke to Chapman when she says: "It may seem to anyone who doesn't know about the matter that vocal prayer doesn't go with contemplation;

but I know that it does. Pardon me, but I want to say this: I know there are many persons who while praying vocally . . . are raised by God to sublime contemplation without their striving for anything or understanding how. It's because of this that I insist so much, daughters, upon your reciting vocal prayer well."[31] Even if we do not pray the formal, vocal prayer in the way we used to, as St. John of the Cross pointed out. Saint Teresa wants to suggest that the manner in which we pray formal, vocal prayers changes and becomes the very doorway through which we move into the silence of contemplation.

Vocal prayer leads us from the surface of the said to the silence that overflows as saying. Herein is the difference between vocal prayer as mind-numbing babble and vocal prayer that manifests sacred Presence, into Whose silence we disappear in self-forgetful love. It would seem that St. Teresa differs slightly from her younger protégé, St. John of the Cross. For St. John of the Cross, our former way of praying dries up. For St. Teresa of Avila, it opens up. It is not a question of who is right. Some people identify more with one than the other.

Boredom is something like a vase that we inherited long ago from a tedious aunt and do not know quite what to do with. Spiritual growth will change what we make of this vase; not something kept idly atop the cupboard but a fragile treasure; not so much empty as deeply receptive, revealing by this empty openness nothing painted in words but nonetheless one of life's great oracles:

> "Beauty is truth, truth beauty"—that is all
> Ye know on earth, and all ye need to know.[32]

The abbess of Crewe doubtless scanned these famous lines from yet another poet as her edges were ground smooth by prayer.

SIX

Creative Disintegration

Depression, Panic, and Awareness

You shall not fear the terrors of the night.
—Psalm 90:5

It is more serious to lose hope than to sin.
—St. John of Karpathos

A REVERENT JOY

It hurt even to wake up in the morning. Physically Josh looked fine, but emotionally he was black and blue. The sleepless hours in bed at night were an ordeal; for "the terrors of the night" (Ps 90:5) prevented the self-forgetful release into sleep. To explain to his friends the circles under his eyes he was fond of quoting Huckleberry Finn: "I didn't sleep much. I couldn't, somehow, for thinking."[1] When morning finally came, it took him twenty to thirty minutes to peel his blank stare off the wall and get off the edge of the bed. Shaving could take another half hour. It took several years for depression's clamp to tighten its grip enough to make Josh want to see his doctor. The doctor recommended medication and then asked him, "Have you ever thought of meditation?" [2] The question threw him.

Many years ago Josh had indeed had a well-established practice of silent prayer, but it fell by the wayside. He began praying after he came across a simple book, *The Way of the Pilgrim*, which moved him deeply. It is the tale of a Russian pilgrim's discovery of the Jesus Prayer as the response to Scripture's invitation "Pray always" (1 Thes 5:17). He used to sit completely still and pray the Jesus Prayer for a half hour first thing in the morning, as well as when he cycled to and from work. But after several months his initial enthusiasm went flat. Josh replaced his regular praying of the Jesus Prayer with the TV remote; he would flip obsessively through countless satellite channels, blinking bleary-eyed at all the television programs he didn't really want to watch, yet halfhoping that the very next program would give him some sense of being alive. So he flipped around and around TV channels. Meanwhile his contemplative practice fell down somewhere behind the sofa and remained there a few years.

Josh took his doctor's advice and returned to his former practice of silent prayer in the mornings as well as when cycling to and from work. After a few months, he recounted the following extraordinary event: "The Jesus Prayer quickly led me back to the monotony that had defeated me some years ago. But I stayed with it this time. One night I fell asleep praying the Jesus Prayer, then, when I awoke in the middle of the night as I usually do, I felt a cleansing warmth welling up within me. The name, 'Jesus' was a living presence streaming within me. Something inside started being freed up and I started to weep in this cleansing warmth and compassion. I wept much of the night and awoke in the morning still praying the Jesus Prayer. For the first time in many months I awoke with no anxiety but instead a reverent joy. When I went downstairs for breakfast, my sister had come over. She said, 'What's wrong with you? You look happy.' That was the first and last time anything 'spiritual' happened like that, but I'm more or less faithful to the periods of praying the Jesus Prayer. Even if there are no more experiences like this one, there is still something deeply attractive that keeps drawing me back, a sense of being just on the verge of finding life again."

Josh's ordeal with depression and anxiety provides a concrete example of the previous chapter's description of how deepening concentration accompanies expanding awareness, the way a pebble dropped in a pond sends out ever-widening rings. For our purposes, the practical value of Josh's ordeal with depression is that his depression did not in fact clear up in either the short or medium term. It took quite some time for medication and meditation to mop up the kicked-over bucket of a decade's despair.

But nothing was wasted in this period of depression, for ultimately the ordeal showed him where the "pearl of great price" lay buried (Mt 13:46–46), and it enables us to see how our contemplative practice can deepen and expand endlessly, even in the midst of intense emotional struggle such as depression and anxiety.

It is easier than we think to use spirituality to keep at bay what spirituality will one day make us face head-on: our own personal struggles. The threads of Providence are braided right into the knots of our own aversion, despair, depression, and panic. Insofar as we discover the Life (Jn 14:6) that is revealed on the contemplative path, we will encounter at some point the dark side of the emotions. Living through, praying in the midst of, and ultimately seeing through our emotions is crucial to learning what this ordeal has to teach. This is not to say that our emotions are not real. They are just not real in the way we normally think they are. Our emotions are transparent to the Light that grounds them. Whether our emotions are dark and crippling or enlivening, Light shines within darkness and Light shines within light. We cannot light a candle that is already lit; trying to is a great waste of time. We simply need to look into a radically decluttered mind and see this Light of awareness for ourselves.

MOODS AND THEIR TRAILS OF THOUGHT

Josh's experience of the warming and cleansing effects of the Jesus Prayer enabled him to see, as it were, by torchlight.

His growth in the practice of contemplation, however, did not begin by getting rid of his depression, as though contemplation were an aerosol spray that masks a bad odor. His practice slowly began its work by allowing him gradually to see the relationship between mood and the trail of negative thinking and how this contributed to the momentum and weight of consistently low mood and energy.[3]

Years of depression had distorted his view of himself and the world around him. For example, he considered himself to be disliked by everybody. In point of fact he had a number of devoted friends, and in general people did like him for his kindness and quick wit. While he could understand rationally that he had friends, there were always several running commentaries in his head that shaped his impressions as they came into awareness. First, he felt his friends didn't actually like him; a reflex response would whisper to him that these people were just being courteous out of the kindness of their hearts. Second, if ever there were a conflict or misunderstanding—if someone got angry or frustrated with him—the same reflex response would interpret this to mean total breakdown of the relationship: they would never speak again. Third, if things were not going well in his life, there had to be someone else to blame for it: there had to be an enemy.

Occasionally he had suicidal thoughts. He felt reasonably sure that he would never act on these thoughts because he could never do this to his parents. Moreover, because he felt himself such a burden to others, he didn't want to trouble people with planning his funeral or sorting through his personal affairs, cancelling credit cards, closing bank accounts, and so on.

By far the most crippling and subtle thought that shaped much of his lifestyle and demeanor was the thought that he didn't count. Part of this came from being a middle child. His older sibling was a near-genius as well as a tennis player with a national ranking that got him into Stanford University. The younger sibling was born with spina bifida. All the family dynamics focused either on his older sibling's brilliant successes or on his younger sibling's unquestionable needs. Josh participated happily in this family dynamic. He would not have had it any other way. Just as well, for the family dynamic could not have been any other way. Josh grew up and left home for university with the sense that he was invisible or trapped behind the wallpaper of a room full of family and friends. This family dynamic transferred quite naturally into his spiritual life. Josh was dutiful in the practice of his faith, but felt God was distant and really didn't care about him. He said, "I feel cut off from people, from God, from everything, like I'm living inside a sealed envelope." He said he knew something was wrong when he was reading the words of the Carmelite author Blessed Elizabeth of the Trinity, on accepting God's love: "Let yourself be loved."[4] He said, "I knew her words were meant for me, but I felt absolutely nothing."

The inner calm that is slowly cultivated by the practice of contemplation encourages and enables us to see right into the mind. In a previous chapter, St. Diadochos told us that the mind was like the sea into whose depths we can see: "When the sea is calm, fishermen can scan its depths and therefore hardly any creature moving in the water escapes their notice. But when the sea is disturbed by the winds it hides beneath its turbid and agitated waves what it was happy to reveal when it was smiling and calm; and then the fishermen's skill and cunning prove vain."[5] Josh's practice of contemplation did not cause his depression to disperse, at least not at first. While he claimed that the cleansing warmth welling up within him never happened again, the experience seemed to integrate him into the experience. This is precisely why we are considering Josh. His depression remained for some time; however, his practice of contemplation continued to deepen and allowed him to see the thoughts and thought-clusters that maintained low mood and low energy. Being able to see the thoughts and thought-clusters in turn helped loosen the grip of depression. Even while depression remained present to a certain extent, its grip loosened considerably.

Josh's depression set in over a period of several years. When he first returned to the practice of contemplation, he had no awareness of the role that thoughts and clusters of thoughts played in maintaining the depression. Growth in awareness of these thoughts was precisely one of the fruits of that single experience of the Jesus Prayer as a living presence streaming within him.

Saint Hesychios likens the practice of awareness and interior stillness to a spider on its web. "If you wish to engage in spiritual warfare, let that little animal, the spider, always be your example for stillness of heart; otherwise you will not be as still in your intellect as you should be. If during your struggle you are as still in your soul as is the spider, you will be blessed by the Holy Spirit."[6] The spider is most aware when it is most still. As soon as anything lands in its web, the spider suddenly springs into action in order to wrap the insect in silk. And so with our thoughts, the more we are still, the more we are alert and aware. This awareness is precisely what Josh is drawn into.

He could now see how certain thoughts would cluster together: the feeling that he did not matter to anyone caused him to withdraw, which caused him in turn to feel isolated. Feeling isolated, he lost interest in life. A depressed mood moved in on the heels of this train of thought and became a permanent resident. However, walking by torchlight, dwelling in this circle of the light of awareness, Josh eventually became able to observe thoughts as they rise and fall. Instead of getting caught up in reactive commentary on the fact that depression is present, he can look right into the depression and say "Oh, look, I'm blaming again"; or "There's the thought 'Nobody likes me'"; or "Look at how I run myself down before anybody else gets the opportunity." Like a spider on its web, Josh is aware of anything that lands in the silk-spun web of awareness. This gets Josh out of a reactive mode and into a receptive mode of meeting inner conflict. Once Josh allows depression to be present, instead of resenting or panicking in the presence of depression, he can live in peace with the fact that depression is present, without feeling a need to comment that it should be gone if it does not happen to be gone. Josh became aware that there was something within that is untouched by depression.

Josh had no further spiritual breakthroughs, but he still has many decades before him. While his depression has never cleared up entirely, his life definitely has more vitality and joy. "I occasionally experience peak moments of real happiness," he says. "But frankly I would simply prefer to live consistently out of my practice than to have these peaks that will soon become dark valleys, because my practice is rock solid and always still amid the peaks and valleys." Josh bows in reverent gratitude for whatever light breaks through the clouds.

THE SHOULDERS OF DISTRACTION

Allison's depression was a large trough of reactive depression. In the course of one week, two events pinched her like a crab's claw. First, right in front of their home she saw her son narrowly escape being hit by a car. Second, thoroughly expecting to be promoted to senior vice president at the investment bank where she had worked for the last thirteen years, she was informed that as a result of the bank's recent takeover by a larger bank, she would be let go in two weeks' time.

While she knew there was depression on all sides of the family, nothing could have prepared her for depression's crushing grip on her. She found herself waking during the night in a state of breathless panic. "The only thing I can compare it with is driving along in a car that suddenly throws on its brakes." Her breath became short and shallow, and she felt certain she was going to die. During the day she was lethargic, unable to focus, and the panic changed from the feeling of being hurled out of sleep by the slamming-on of brakes to a persistent rattle. This rattling panic and depression became the two pincers that held her captive.

In contrast to Josh, Allison was more than adept at contemplative prayer. Now in her late fifties, Allison had spent most of her twenties as a Cistercian (Trappistine) nun. When she hit twenty-nine years of age, her up-to-then-undoubted (yet untried by interior struggle) monastic vocation began to deflate until all the air had escaped. The balloon of her vocation now lay flat as latex gloves. She left the monastery. She took with her, however, not only the love of all her sisters and impeccable

French but also the spiritual disciplines she had learned during her nine years with this community: simplicity of life, praying the psalms, and sitting in prayerful silence. She continued to live many of these values, adapting them to married life, motherhood, and a career with an investment bank.

Somehow she had taken the view that just because she was much more than a beginner in the practice of contemplation she should not be having the emotional struggles she was currently having; after all her son was perfectly fine, and she had nearly decided to take early retirement from the bank anyway. The reactive depression had no rational basis (she concluded) now that the initial shock of it was over. Moreover, since leaving the monastery she had continued to pray for nearly two hours each day, and she had a nourishing liturgical life in her parish community and the emotional support of a like-minded husband. "Furthermore," she chided herself, "if there is a certain level of spiritual realization, shouldn't a person be able to avoid things like bouts of depression and panic attacks?" Owing to some glitch in her logic, she had decided that deeply prayerful people don't struggle; that prayer is a way around struggle. She could not see why this battle with depression and panic should be happening to her. But the pathless path of prayer knows only how to move through struggle; and the only way through is through—not around, over, under, or alongside, but through.

Thus she found herself on the horns of a dilemma: either she could sit in silence and risk facing the gale-force headwinds of this ordeal, or she could flee from silence and be chased by the tailwinds of depression and panic. Being exhausted by the latter, she decided (after several weeks) to try the former. And so she simply returned to her practice of sitting in silence, waiting to be tossed and buffeted by headwinds of inner chaos. She sat in silent prayer. Nothing happened.

Like Tolstoy's Ivan Ilyich, she "looked for her customary fear of death" but could not find it.[7] There was a deep peace, which she could not deny. Nor could she deny that depression was still present. In certain respects, the depression was like a storm cloud that thundered with fear-driven rage. Rage at what? She could not quite say, and it did not seem to matter. If she wandered away from her prayer-word-united-with-her-breath, the depression began its fear-rattle. If, however, she remained immersed in her practice the depression was simply there, no tailwinds, no being tossed around. By itself depression posed no threat, but if it became an object to which she reacted with commentary, it would rage and storm. Stillness was the only way forward.

In other respects, the depression was not like a storm cloud at all but more like a dye that colored with its freezing blue the entire cloth of personality: simple emotions, appetite, interest in life, self-confidence, the ability to read and write with focus, clarity, and pace, the ability to get out of bed and remain out of bed for the entire day.

It was easier for her to get through the day if she lived out of her practice as much as possible and engaged each moment of the day while remaining in her prayer-word-united-with-her-breath, inhaling and exhaling each moment just as it came. For those fairly new to the practice of contemplation, like Josh, this would be a very tall order, but for the more seasoned, like Allison, who knows from experience the steady gaze into the open countryside of the mind, this is the way to advance ever more deeply into that countryside, where she can breathe and see and live.

The fourteenth-century anonymous English author of *The Cloud of Unknowing* suggests that instead of pushing away or clinging to thoughts and images that appear in our awareness, whether distracting or attracting, we should simply "look over their shoulder."[8] This ingeniously playful advice requires a serious and cultivated inner awareness. Indeed, the author of *The Cloud* speaks of that season of practice that St. Hesychios calls the "moon circling the heart's firmament."[9] In order to look over the shoulders of distraction, our practice must allow several things to take place in one effortless effort. First, in order to look over the shoulders of distraction we have to allow the distraction to be present, when normally we would tend to push away or cling to anything we are aware of. Second, we have to be interiorly silent enough to notice that distractions have shoulders, so to speak, that can be looked over. Third, in order to look over the shoulders of distraction we have to meet distractions with stillness instead of commentary. Fourth, meeting distractions with stillness instead of with commentary implies that not only do we allow distractions to be present but we also allow them to help us steady our gaze as we "look over their shoulders, as it were, searching for something else."[10] This advice from the author of *The Cloud* teaches us a new way of being present to distractions and moods. In Allison's and Josh's case it is depression.

In one of his sermons, Meister Eckhart says, "What used to be a hindrance now helps you most."[11] Our preference would be that depression would be gone, but if it happens to be present we want to look right into it until we can look straight through it. In this way even depression can help steady our inner gaze just as much as feelings of inner recollection, though clearly one is preferable to the other.

Allison's practice is seasoned enough that she can simply be present and be aware of the depression. Her next step in this sojourn is to shift her attention from the depression (the object of her awareness) to the awareness itself, to what is aware of depression. This flowing vastness of simple awareness, what St. Hesychios calls "the sun rising in the heart,"[12] is untouched by depression just as it is untouched by time, by age, by pain, fear, anger, or greed, or by anything else—though simple awareness is never separate from any of these any more than a spoke of a wheel is separated from its hub. The spoke is not the hub, yet the hub centers all the spokes. When we shift the attention from the spoke of depression to the hub of simple awareness the mind immediately becomes expansively still, even though depression may still be present. This is easier said than done; because the thinking mind has such momentum, it will try to make an object out of this grounding awareness and make us think we need to become aware of awareness. This is not what we are talking about. We are talking about the stillness of simple awareness and gazing into that. That which gazes is also simple, vast awareness. All objects that appear and disappear in awareness arise from and lead back to this grounding awareness. The best practical response to this is simply to be in your practice. Allison found that she could do this. During the next couple of weeks, her relationship with the presence of depression began to change from being a relationship with something that sought her out in order to victimize her to being a relationship with something that pointed beyond itself into the very silence she sought, the sun rising in the heart.[13]

ON NOT FLOSSING AND BRUSHING TOO MUCH

From adolescence, Margot has flossed and brushed her teeth several times a day or more. When dining out, she could not wait until she returned home to floss and brush her teeth but would instead excuse herself from the table, retire to the ladies' room, and floss and brush her teeth. In fact she did not brush her teeth as much as scour them.

Her father had been a dentist, and, while she had no awareness of this as a child, her father had a cruel streak that ran deep: "If you have good habits of oral hygiene, your teeth should last you all your life," he would preach. If she ever had a cavity that needed filling, he gave just under the normal amount of anesthetic; the pain would help teach her to stay away from sugary food and drinks. As she sat in his dentist's chair, he would pinch her knee until it hurt and then not let her go. When she asked him to stop, he simply said the pain in her knee would take her mind off the pain of the drilling. She came to despise him to the point of once actually wishing he were dead. Indeed, her father dropped dead of a heart attack the next day. The autopsy confirmed he had advanced heart disease, but Margot believed she caused his death. Thus she began to floss and floss and floss her teeth and then brush and brush and brush her teeth seven times a day. She flossed and brushed so much that her gums became inflamed and bled. She brushed so hard that by the second or third day her toothbrush's bristles had so fanned out as to render it useless. She carried floss, tooth-picks, toothbrushes, and toothpaste in her purse. If she were someplace where she simply could not floss and brush (which was rare), she would become breathless with panic. As she aged, her guilt for causing her father's death grew, and so did her panic. Knowing that heart disease killed her father and not her wish that he were dead did little to prevent Margot from being completely obsessed with brushing her teeth.

Margot attends a centering prayer group that meets once a week. She is very much a beginner. In fact, she does not sit in silent prayer apart from these group meetings as the others do. But she does hope to work up the courage to do the same as the others. Silent prayer once a week is better than nothing. Eating nourishing food once a week is better than nothing. But ideally we nourish our bodies every day and so likewise we should nourish our spirit.

Margot is preoccupied with her feelings of inadequacy and is convinced that this is all God sees in her. Quite understandably, silent prayer is as difficult for her as it is attractive. While she understands the theory of the practice of contemplation, when she does sit in silence she is beset by thought upon thought upon thought about what she considers to be her shortcomings (including feeling responsible for her father's death), leaving her with a very constricted awareness.

While our struggles with compulsive thinking and behavior might not be as habituated as Margot's, we can likely profit by the wisdom of two teachers of silent prayer who address struggles with obsessive thinking and behavior, St. John of the Cross and the author of *The Cloud of Unknowing*.

In one of his letters, St. John of the Cross consoles a woman who suffers from scruples, a type of obsessive compulsive disorder that besets spirituality.[14] The result is a sense of feeling plagued by an irrationally based sense of sin that prevents us from any sense of a living faith in God's indwelling presence. If one changed the details, it is easy to see that St. John of the Cross's advice is as relevant to Margot as to the woman he wrote to in 1590.[15]

Saint John of the Cross would hope to get Margot to reshape her cognitive habits by working with her negative thoughts. Thus he would encourage her to focus not on her faults and failings but instead on the Indwelling Presence. "Let your care and esteem for this be so great that nothing else will matter to you or receive your attention, whether it may concern some affliction or some other disturbing memories."[16] Moreover, St. John of the Cross knows that our own negative thinking about ourselves tends to manifest itself in being hypercritical of the faults of others. Hence, he advises (as though it's easy to do): "And if there be faults in the house during these days, pass over them."[17]

Margot receives from time to time the sacrament of reconciliation or confession. For people with sensitive consciences rooted in abuse, this can be excruciatingly painful.

Here, too, St. John of the Cross thinks she should exercise caution and keep the confession of sins general and not go picking tediously through them. By this advice John shows he is sensitive to the fact that some people get so wrapped up in their own shortcomings instead of the Indwelling Presence that they can think of little else but their sins. So John encourages the woman he is counseling to do positive things that bring her joy. He mentions in particular reading, praying, and rejoicing in God.[18] Surely there are other possibilities as well.

Saint John of the Cross is aware of how people can unwittingly co-opt religion into enhancing their sense of bondage instead of liberation. His point is to get people like Margot out of their world of inner chatter, even if it means brushing our teeth less often.

The author of *The Cloud of Unknowing* is likewise concerned to teach the perils of preoccupation with one's faults and failings. The author of *The Cloud* asks if Mary Magdalene remained fixated on her own past or if she instead focused on God.[19] "Did she therefore come down from the heights of desire [for God] into the depths of her sinful life, and search in the foul stinking fen and dunghill of her sins, sorting through them one by one in every detail, and sorrowing and weeping for each of them separately? No, certainly she did not. And why? Because God let her know by his inward grace in her soul that in that

way she would never succeed. For in that way she was
more likely to have aroused in herself the possibility of sin-
ning again. . . . And so she hung her love and her longing
desire on this cloud of unknowing."[20] The author of *The
Cloud* is saying that Mary Magdalene, having repented of
her past sins, did not keep reminding herself of them.
Instead she "hung her love on the cloud of unknowing."
By this he means that she returned to her practice of contemplation instead of obsessive commenting on her past
faults and failings. Had she continued to be preoccupied
by her misdeeds, she would have been less likely to move
beyond the mental habits that undergirded her moral
struggles. Margot's struggles were not with sin, but nevertheless the observations of *The Cloud*'s author shed light
on her predicament: the more she indulged mental habits
of guilt and shame stemming from her abusive father and
his untimely death, the more she would floss and brush
and floss and brush. Her refuge became her contemplative
practice, which gradually nurtured a positive habit of letting go and looking straight through the thoughts that fed
the behavior that left her gums inflamed and bleeding.
Looking through these obsessive thoughts instead of
running from them or rehearsing them yet again, Margot
herself soon broke through, much as Mary Magdalene did.
Pauline Matarasso's poem sums up the breakthroughs of
both Margot and Mary Magdalene:

Reaching her arms so high
she thrust them through
to peg love's laundry in the sky
and white against the blue
her banners flew.[21]

Both the author of *The Cloud of Unknowing* and St. John of the Cross are well aware that obsessive thinking and behavior are healed by working with the mental habits that undergird unhealthy thoughts and behavior. The spiritual discipline of contemplation will target these mental habits. Hence, St. John of the Cross's famous aphorism "What we need most in order to make progress is to be silent before this great God with our cravings and with our tongue, the language he hears best is silent love."[22]

BATTLES IN THE HEALTHY SOUL

For some reason we think that spiritual progress is marked by lack of struggle in life. The purpose of this chapter is to emphasize that this is simply not the case. Spiritual progress is learning to confront struggle in a new way so that we don't struggle with the fact that life is fraught with struggle. But the practice of contemplation will expose us to many things we would rather not see but need to see if we are going to grow. Even something as potentially debilitating as depression or obsessive-compulsive behavior finds healing salve in the practice of contemplation.

Saint Teresa of Avila was amazed to discover that in her own daily life interior struggle and deep, bedrock peace often occurred together. She states with her customary authority: "Just because the soul sits in perpetual peace does not mean that the faculties of sense and reason do, or the passions. There are always wars going on in the other dwellings of the soul. There is no lack of trials and exhaustion. But these battles rarely have power any more to unseat the soul from her place of peace."[23]

Stillness calms and soothes even such battles as depression and obsessive-compulsive behavior. These, too, can be vehicles by which the mystery we call God breaks through and shines in awareness.

SEVEN

Sharp Trials in the Intellect

Consider yourselves fortunate when all kinds of trials come your way, because you know that when your faith succeeds in facing such trials, the result is the ability to endure.
—James 1:2–3

"VERY LOVING LIGHT"

Ego is often maligned as some sort of table-pounding ogre, or a spoiled brat who throws all the toys out of the pram when things don't go its way. While ego certainly has its bad days, it is also quite happy to charm the birds out of the trees, especially if it helps it enjoy the adulation of a coterie of admirers.

Spirituality is champagne for the ego. Cork after cork pops as ego guzzles enthusiastically while reading up on what phase of the spiritual life it is in, what doorways of prayer it has pranced through; or it insists that it is "spiritual, not religious," or "religious, not spiritual"—whatever the trendy sound bite of the day is that will keep it at the center of all drama or trauma. Ego does not have to be unpleasant or tiresome, but it does need to be center stage.

Ego, therefore, does not take boredom lying down. It has a way of stealing the keys to the car so that it can drive excitedly, even recklessly, revving the engines of self-centeredness as it barrels along for all to see and hear—anything to keep boredom at bay.

In a previous chapter we considered how boredom serves a liberating role in the spiritual life, signaling the onset of contemplation. Boredom serves to pry loose ego's grip on whatever it is holding onto, and it holds onto whatever it can. But if we are set on becoming free, and not just on feeling secure or winning arguments, the velcro mesh of our lives must be pried loose from ego's many, tiny hooks. Ego cannot do this itself; it clings with such tenacity. We can only receive contemplation's gift; ego knows only how to take.

Once we have become acclimated to the liberating role of boredom in our prayer life, indeed come to prefer this desert over the fleshpots of religious experience, as our prayer life may once have been, there is yet more freeing up and deepening that the practice of contemplation will continue to do. But we may well not see this deepening; more likely we see our prayer life crumbling, yet all the while there is deepening taking place as we are exposed to things within ourselves that we would rather not see, but need to see. This humbling self-knowledge is a crucial component of the deepening of our practice. Saint John of the Cross insists that this light we are filled with is "very loving light,"[1] but for lengthy stretches of the spiritual journey, as our practice deepens, this "very loving light" enables us to see aspects of ourselves that we would rather not see but nevertheless bear our name. This humbling self-knowledge is the direct result of the inflow of light into our awareness. As when opening the curtains in a room we have not been in for some time, the light exposes all manner of dirt and dust. The dirt and dust were always there, but there was not light sufficient to see. But St. John of the Cross never wavers from his conviction that this light is not simply luminous but also "very loving light."

In this season of our prayer life—a season that can last for quite a long time—what the light illumines is not altogether pleasant. It all depends on how much of the mesh ego has its hooks into. One of Flannery O'Connor's more unfortunate main characters, the bigoted Mrs. May in "Greenleaf," is illumined by self-knowledge in a rather brutal way that she does not happen to live through. Mrs. May does not encounter light so much as she is gored by light as it comes racing toward her like the Sun of Justice, in the form of a bull. As the bull gores her, she has "the look of a person whose sight has suddenly been restored but now finds the light unbearable."[2]

The ordeal with loving light has no other purpose than to free us by pointing out what our minds cling to. Both Flannery

O'Connor and St. John of the Cross indicate that this is a deeper cleansing and release. The real shackles of the heart pertain more to intellect: the mind's laziness, its scorn, its pre-occupation with reputation. Saint John of the Cross learns something quite similar from watching wood burn. He says that the divine light "has the same effect on a soul that fire has on a log of wood."[3] The fire attributes to wood its own properties. While the wood continues to have properties characteristic of wood such as weight and quantity, it takes on properties characteristic of fire: it is hot and it heats; it is brilliant and also illumines; it is dry and it is drying. The fire produces all these effects as it gradually transforms the wood into flame, the union of Creator and creature, in such a way that we now have wooden flame or flaming wood. Gradually, the fire makes the wood "as beautiful as it is itself."[4] With this process, however, there is deeper liberation and, as St. John of the Cross implies, deeper pain, for this liberation targets not our greed, gluttony, or lust but the intellect; this is a more painful liberation. "At this stage persons suffer from sharp trials in the intellect, severe dryness and distress in the will, and from the burdensome knowledge of their own miseries in the memory, for their spiritual eye gives them a very clear picture of themselves.... They find relief in nothing, nor does any thought console them, nor can they even raise the heart to God, so oppressed are they by this flame."[5] Through all of this, however, the fire remains loving; it's just that what love draws out is unsightly and for sometimes long stretches of time difficult to bear.

SHARP TRIALS IN THE INTELLECT

Saint Gregory of Nyssa says in his *Life of Moses* that any concept that attempts to define God "becomes an idol of God and does not make God known."[6] We have an insatiable and natural need to conceptualize. But in order to know God, the Christian contemplative tradition insists on the "unknowing" that is higher (or deeper) than conceptual knowledge that the practice of contemplation cultivates. Saint Thomas Aquinas claims that "the end of our knowing is to know God as something unknown."[7] To know God the mind must be still (Ps 46:10). Initially (and this can last quite some time) to be drawn into this unknowing makes previous trials seem like mere child's play; for the compulsive need to conceptualize everything in sight does not relent. When we are drawn into the presence of God with our conceptual mind gunning its engines, we are in for a rather rude awakening. In his *Homilies on the Beatitudes*, St. Gregory of Nyssa likens it to stepping onto a "slippery, steep rock that affords no basis for our thoughts."[8] With nothing to hold onto, the conceptual mind cannot stabilize itself. Saint Gregory likens this encounter with God to being on the edge of a mountain precipice. Finding no toehold or handhold, "the mind has nothing it can grasp, neither place nor time, neither space nor any other thing which offers our mind something to grasp hold of, but, slips from all sides from what it fails to grasp, in dizziness and confusion."[9]

We may have known this liberating purification previously, but it focused more on the surface faculties of the soul, such as greed, gluttony, or lust. Not that these struggles did not give us a run for our money, but in classical Christian theology they are considered less spiritually dangerous. While struggles with these may generate a greater media interest, they are, in the ancient view of things, nearer the surface of the soul and produce more garden-variety suffering than the much sharper pain of confronting more spiritual, and therefore more dangerous, intellectual sins such as pride, envy, judgmentalism, or vainglory. When the loving flame of God sets about healing these sins of the intellect it is more painful because they are more spiritual, and we become painfully aware of just how beset by them we are. Indeed we are progressing along the path of holiness, but as a result we become aware of just how filled we are with deeply rooted intellectual habits that blind us to the loving light. As St. John of the Cross sees it, this is perfectly consistent with how wood takes on the qualities of fire. Before the wood becomes wooden flame—completely one with fire—the wood spits and hisses and oozes in preparation for becoming all flame. As part of the process of healing we become acutely aware of just how filled we are with arrogance, envy, preoccupation with our reputation, judgmentalism. Indeed these characteristics were all there within us, but we were at most only vaguely aware of them; now the living flame of love is drawing them out and placing them in our sight. The problem is that this stage of growth in humbling self-knowledge is singularly painful, with the result that we feel we are falling to pieces when in fact we are becoming one with the living flame of love. As when our prayer was beset by boredom, there is no time limit on these "sharp trials in the intellect." These trials are intertwined with the tangles of Providence and are tailor made for each person, but the following are common enough places to undergo them: our relationship with beauty, knowledge, spiritual advancement, idealism—each presents a different opportunity to observe the grasping, clinging mind (this list is by no means exhaustive).

We need as much beauty in our lives as possible, but this trial can show itself in our relationship with beauty when the grasping, craving mind fragments the perception of beauty in such a way that we try to cling to it. This may show itself as a powerful attempt to possess the beautiful object or simply fantasize that we do. Until our relationship with beauty is cleansed and set free simply to gaze into and reverence Beauty, we will not be in a right relationship with Beauty. This trial in the intellect has for its sole purpose the expansion of our capacity to realize the depths of our immersion in Beauty, even in the most seemingly mundane contexts.

Study and learning are spiritual disciplines much esteemed in the Christian contemplative tradition (as they are in many religious traditions). When this discipline is being strengthened and purified to make the discursive mind a better servant of God, we become aware of a not-so-subtle tendency to show off how much we have come to know in all our reading and study. This need not be a public display; we can look down on people less well-read than we are in such a way that they don't even notice it. When this form of pride or arrogance is being healed we are not only painfully aware of just how much we do this, but it can be painful to study in the way we did before. We find we cannot even read; for it hurts too much to see our intellectual arrogance so clearly.

It is common enough that a certain isolation infects our fidelity to the spiritual life in such a way that we look down on others for not having journeyed as far along the spiritual path as we have. We do not need any evidence to back this up with. We look down on others from nothing other than dint of mental habit.

Christianity proposes lofty values, which we interiorize and genuinely attempt to live out. We believe them with our whole heart. If this commitment is not balanced by an operative knowledge of how much we fall short of them, we will likely struggle a great deal with the fact that others fall short of the ideal as well. We do not see that under the veneer of our idealism we are judging other people. This judgment is usually based on our own ignorance of the basic fact that we do not know the inner recesses of the human heart, which only God can see. The person whom we judge may very well be doing better than we are. But this is not the point. The point is to convince ourselves that we are better than they are. We arrive at this conclusion pretty swiftly, precisely because we have very little in the way of facts to lead us to it.

When we become aware by the light of grace to what extent we flare our nostrils in condescension at how unadvanced other people are, the mental pain is so excruciating we can only take refuge in the Jesus Prayer, or whatever our practice happens to be. It is the one safe place.

These are just some of the mental habits that are involved in what St. John of the Cross calls "sharp trials in the intellect." They are more painful than the garden-variety suffering we know when this very "loving light" illumines our gluttony, greed, or lust. We become aware of the mental habits of the intellect not because we are moving into darkness but, on the contrary, because of our increasing proximity to this very loving light. The initial result of this growth in humbling self-knowledge, initiated and consummated by grace, is the not-so-consoling sense that our life is falling apart with nowhere to turn. No logician, saint, or scholar can convince us during the years of these sharp trials that this is actually growth, for the evidence available to us suggests that we have gone way off course or else we would not be hurting the way we are at the sight of what we see in ourselves.

IMPASSE

Brian was both intellectually gifted and genuinely longed for holiness. He tried to keep this tightly under wraps, but among friends in medical school, believer and nonbeliever alike recognized how important his spiritual life was for him. His attempts to be self-effacing about all this did nothing but confirm in the eyes of those who knew him that, despite his lack of years, he was a holy man. Moreover, his intellectual gifts eventually led him to the top of his field as a surgeon, yet no one was surprised by his announcement that instead of continuing in private practice he would join an international charitable organization whose mission it was to bring medical help to the world's most impoverished. Brian soon found himself in a Congolese village, heading up a small and undersupplied medical team.

Prayer and daily Mass had always been pillars of his adult life. Due to the presence of Catholic missionaries in the town, he could continue this practice that nourished him spiritually. He rose early each morning to pray in silence, and Mass was just a short walk from the clinic. Evenings often presented another time for prayer as he joined the missionary community for evening prayer and meditation.

The physical simplicity of his life was a bit more than he had bargained for, in spite of the fact that all the "Europeans" were somewhat catered to when it came to diet and personal hygiene. But despite these accommodations he found the lifestyle rigorous. While none of the details of the living arrangements were quite what he had imagined (they were far worse than anything he could have imagined), he felt he was answering a call he had been hearing since before he entered medical school. He found himself happy though physically stretched.

After a year Brian was offered a midlevel administrative position that involved a much-needed coordination of efforts of all medical teams among the various international medical organizations throughout the Congo. He had a head for administration and valued this opportunity to liaise with groups from all over the world. Very soon into this new job, however, a trial beset him. He was very quickly growing to loathe his immediate boss, who was unpredictable, unreliable, and incompetent. For the first few months Brian was able to find solace in his prayer life, but for some reason this, too, began to dry up like every-thing else in the Congolese terrain.

By virtue of his gentle personality Brian was not accustomed to hating anyone. Most frustrating of all, however, was the way his anger at his boss had taken over his prayer life. Over many years, Brian had cultivated a strong interior silence. He knew its nuances, its many faces; he knew how silence both manifested and led to the core of all. Now the silence was gone. Anger replaced it. Not only anger at his boss's monumental incompetence but also anger that he was letting his anger get to him. His was a type of anger that comes like a worm from the past, bores its way through the wood of the present, and threatens to devour the future. Brian did not even know that he had any history with anger that could come from the past and hold the present captive.

Brian was always thankful that his father pushed him hard. Or so he thought. He knew that his father wanted the best for him and he could never become the man his father wanted him to be by slacking off in school, athletics, or summer jobs. His father was demanding, but it was for Brian's own good. Brian knew this. Or so he thought. He could not have gotten into medical school without someone always pushing him. He was sure it was for his own good. Or so he thought. During this current crisis with his boss, Brian found himself telling himself over and over that his father's high expectations were just what he needed to make something of himself. As proof of this, he needed only to remind himself that he was now starting to move up the ranks of his organization. The problem was that anger at his father's domineering manner became a preoccupation that inundated his practice of the Jesus Prayer. Prayer time became an angry rant in his head about how his father had pushed him so hard to succeed. Prayer that had been a mainstay was now an ordeal.

Anger and personal pain often team up together, especially if the pain is old pain. Their bond is all the more indissoluble when they are bound together by a sense of deep, personal loss. What was Brian's loss? Brian's father never regarded him as a person in his own right, with his own emotions, sensations, hopes, and desires. He had no sense that his father esteemed him for who he was. Brian's father was always there to push him, but what Brian wanted from his father was someone always there to steady him, to reassure him. In order to receive his father's approval Brian created a mask. This mask received full and consistent approval from his father, who told Brian that he was genuinely proud of what Brian had made of himself. But *who* Brian was went completely unnoticed by his father.

Brian's first evaluation in the new administrative position came three months into the job. Brian's boss, whom Brian considered unpredictable, unreliable, and incompetent, wrote the report. On balance the report was favorable, but when it came to the section of the report designated for areas of future growth, his boss suggested that in certain areas Brian was unpredictable, unreliable, and not yet entirely competent. But the boss had no doubt that with time and the right sort of mentoring Brian would become predictable, reliable, and competent in every way. When Brian read this he nearly went through the roof.

Externally Brian remained highly functional. Interiorly, however, he felt he was in an impasse: on the one hand, he wanted to leave the organization; on the other, he had made a commitment for five years of service and genuinely liked the work he was doing. Yet something within him was breaking down. His prayer life, which had always sustained him, changed from being a mainstay to being a challenge that showed Brian something he had never seen in himself before: how attached he was to his reputation. In his heart of hearts Brian knew he was doing a good job, and the report actually said this. But this single criticism in one area sent him spinning with anger. Brian knew he was predictable, reliable, and competent. It was his boss who was unpredictable and unreliable, and everyone knew this. But the simple truth of the matter provided no consolation or refuge. He needed the admiration of all, including his boss. His reputation had been questioned, and Brian could not cope with this. As a result Brian found himself in such inner turmoil he thought he could not continue.

Prayer brought no stillness or consolation; prayer was an ordeal between himself and vainglory. It was like praying in the midst of a seventy-mile-per-hour headwind. While Brian found this ordeal excruciating, he could see the truth of the situation. His attachment to being highly thought of by others stemmed from his father's consistent manner of pushing Brian without ever esteeming him for who he was, to say nothing of showing him the slightest bit of affection.

Brian was disciplined enough to stay with his routine of prayer, though it felt much of the time as though he was being pummeled by a right hook from the past and a left jab from the present. Tailor-made for Brian, this trial is just the sort of thing St. John of the Cross is talking about. We find in Brian someone with a dedicated, mature practice of contemplation, supported by regular participation in a praying community. Most important of all, he is faithful to his practice of contemplation whether it's going well or whether all hell is breaking loose. The present trial Brian is going through (attachment to his good reputation) hits at a deep level; it is "a sharp trial of the intellect," as St. John of the Cross calls it. Anybody can suffer from this affliction (Who likes to have their good reputation put into question?), but when it is being targeted by grace for deep liberation from it, it is a sign that a special trial in the intellect is taking place, especially suited to those who are well beyond being beginners on the path of contemplation. Persevering in this grace-initiated trial, instead of retaliating (passively or actively) against those who do not view us as we would have them, is the only thing that will see us through. Saint John of the Cross notes the severe distress and impasse in the will, "and the burdensome knowledge of their own miseries in the memory."[10] Brian's memory was a conduit of pain: the realization of unmet needs he had experienced as a child trying to survive a demanding parent's emotional neediness. Saint John of the Cross says of those in this state: "their spiritual eye gives them a very clear picture of themselves."[11] Brian was keenly aware of just how attached he was to being well thought of by others. While clearly he merited the respect of others, his attachment to having other people think highly of him was rooted in childhood wounds that followed him into adulthood. When Brian's reputation was impugned by his boss's report, it caused this wound to fester to the extent that he could "find relief in nothing."[12]

We should keep in mind that Brian's boss's report was on the whole quite positive. There was just that bit of criticism that mirrored the boss's issues more than they illumined Brian's. With the help of friends, Brian gradually regained perspective and got on with his life as a surgeon-administrator. But as Brian continued to pray in silence, he continued to face the ordeal with vainglory, his attachment to being thought well of by authority and its long trail of history from the past.

M. C. Richards has a most perceptive understanding of the creative potential that lies in the creative disintegration

Brian is going through: "Symptoms of growth may look like breakdown or derangement; the more we are allowed by the love of others and by self-understanding to live through our derangement into the new arrangement, the luckier we are. It is unfortunate when our anxiety over what looks like personal confusion or dereliction blinds us to the forces of liberation at work.[13]

In the months that followed, Brian did what any mature person of prayer would do. He simply stared down the vainglory whenever it presented itself. He discovered that these thoughts were as transparent as all other thoughts, and he made peace with the fact that he would not be at peace for some time, for the "sharp trials of the intellect" do indeed take their sweet time to liberate us by means of what St. John of the Cross insists is "very loving light."[14]

EIGHT

"It Don't Work for Me"

Prayers of Petition and Other Practical Problems

Whatever you ask in my name it will be granted.
—John 14:13

"I reckon it don't work for only just the right kind of people."
—Mark Twain, *The Adventures of
Huckleberry Finn*

The sections of this chapter, randomly arranged, address some of the more frequently asked questions that have come up in the course of my talks and personal correspondence with people. There are many more questions of a practical nature, but the following have surfaced most frequently: the role of intercessory prayer; drowsiness during prayer; praying with icons or statues; not having time to pray; the enneagram and Myers-Briggs Type Indicator; struggling with the fact that nothing ever seems to happen during prayer; changing the prayer word or always saying the prayer word; when charismatic prayer collapses into contemplative prayer; contemplation as an aid to forgiveness.

PRAYER OF PETITION: HUCK FINN
AND DENYS THE AREOPAGITE

Many people on the path of contemplation wonder about
other forms of prayer such as petitionary or intercessory prayer.
The question is not simply theoretical; for when we go deeply
into our practice all other forms of prayer are often integrated
into the simple silence of just being. Yet many contemplatives
also incorporate other forms of prayer such as going to church,
praying the psalms, praying for other people's needs and the
world's needs. There is solid scriptural foundation for all these
forms of prayer. While Jesus routinely went off to some
deserted place to commune with the one he called Abba, Jesus
also asked for things and interceded on behalf of others. Indeed
one would be hard-pressed to find any authoritative teaching
on prayer that would advocate the practice of contemplation
to the exclusion of other forms of prayer.

Huck Finn does not spend much time in prayer of any
sort, yet he wrestles nonetheless with the efficacy of petitionary prayer in *The Adventures of Huckleberry Finn*, and in
these boyish musings we are reminded of something important about petitionary prayer. Jesus says, "Whatever you ask
for in my name, it will be given you" (Jn 14:13). Huck wrestles with this very passage from Scripture and recalls a
number of occasions when people simply do not get what
they ask for: "I says to myself, if a body can get anything

they pray for, why don't Deacon Winn get back the money he lost on pork? Why can't the widow get back her silver snuff-box that was stole? Why can't Miss Watson fat up? No, says I to myself, there ain't nothing in it."[1] Huck is put straight by the widow. He has got to pray for "'spiritual gifts.' ... I must help other people, and do everything I could for other people, and look out for them all the time, and never think about myself. This was including Miss Watson, as I took it. I went out in the woods and turned it over in my mind a long time, but I couldn't see no advantage about it-except for other people—so at last I reckoned I wouldn't worry about it any more, but just let it go."[2] When Huck later realizes that he, too, can be on the receiving end of petitionary prayer, he alters his views. "And then something struck me. I says, now I reckon the widow or the parson or somebody prayed that this bread would find me, and here it has gone and done it. So there ain't no doubt but that there is something in that thing. That is, there's something in it when a body like the widow or the parson prays, but it don't work for me, and I reckon it don't work for only just the right kind."[3] Twain's characters are each one of them flawed, the widow and Miss Watson not least among them, but they are part of a community in which prayer means something. And when Huck stops to consider that he, too, is a part of their prayer, he is drawn, if but for a moment, into a wider circle of community.

The widow was not entirely off her rocker when she said that when we pray to God for things, they are supposed to be spiritual. Not being high church, she did not know that St. Anthony, Saint Joseph, and an army of other saints were delegated for such material requests and even some virtues. Nevertheless, this does not interest Huck, who only wants to be on the receiving end of prayer. But when we petition God for anything over a long period of time, something else begins to happen; we are brought into the depths of God and are joined with God's will. The fourth-century Syrian monk Denys the Areopagite explains how this works. He tells us to "picture ourselves aboard a boat. There are ropes joining it to some rock. We take hold of the rope and pull on it as if we were trying to drag the rock to us when in fact we are hauling ourselves and our boat toward that rock."[4] Denys provides a useful metaphor. We think we know what we need and attempt to bend God to our will, but the more we pull, the closer we are drawn into God's will. Denys continues, "We will not pull down to ourselves that power which is both everywhere and yet nowhere, but by divine reminders and invocations we may commend ourselves to it and be joined to it."[5] We pray to God for this and that. Often these things are important, but gradually we are united to God through our many requests and even in spite of them.

Intercessory prayer poses a similar problem for some people. Are not intercessory prayers and petitions distractions that take us away from the practice of contemplation? In theory they do not rival contemplative practice, but like a prayer word, they can serve to draw our intention as well as our attention to God. In practice, however, most people handle requests to pray for others (intercessory prayer) in one or a combination of two ways. For some, they set aside part of their prayer time explicitly for remembering people who have asked to be remembered in prayer and then they later move into silent prayer. For others it is enough for them to call to mind a need or a request and take it with them into the silence of the heart, without gunning the engines of "now-I'd-like-to-pray-for-so-and-so." There is an intercessory dimension intrinsic to interior silence; for interior silence and compassionate solidarity are of a piece, like spokes leading into the hub of a wheel. Denys likewise perceives this connection between interior silence and interpersonal solidarity as he tries to explain how each part shares the same wholeness. "It is rather like the case of a circle," he says. "The center point of the circle is shared by the surrounding radii."[6] Only on the rim of the wheel of daily life do we appear to be separated from each other, but if we follow each spoke from the rim to the hub, all the spokes of the wheel are one in the center. We each share the same Center. When we are closest to the Creator, we are closest to all creation.

FALLING ASLEEP DURING PRAYER

If dealing with distractions is not bad enough, few things can
be as defeating as battling sleep; perhaps not deep REM sleep,
just the gentle dozing that keeps the head bobbing up and
down. This is one of those areas of struggle about which it is
important not to spiritualize. If you don't get enough deep sleep
during the night, expect prayer time to become nap time. If
you've been blessed with narcolepsy during sermons that merit
that response, it will probably show up in prayer time as well.
Some people stoke themselves with coffee and find that helpful. Others will try to caffeinate themselves into contemplation
and end up with a prayer period of the most apocalyptic sort
imaginable. You simply do the best you can. Old-timers often
have too little good-quality sleep during the night, so any
opportunity for a nap is going to be used for that. Hence, the
importance of finding comfort in the Psalmist: "The Lord gives
to his beloved while they slumber" (Ps 127:2).

There are other times outside official periods of prayer,
which may be used to extend our practice. Virtually any
stretch of time when the discursive (thinking) mind is not
needed (which is a fair bit) will work, as when peeling veg-
etables, vacuuming, ironing, washing the car, gardening,
and so on—all sorts of opportunities exist that we can and
should use in addition to "official" prayer periods. Self-
recrimination is rarely any help.

There is one group of people who experience this sleepy boredom on a regular basis, but not owing to lack of good-quality sleep at night. Certain people have a way of relying heavily on discursive reason. This is quite irrespective of native intelligence or level of formal education. Such people are going to find the practice of contemplation rather tough going because they have a strong habit of thinking about everything (again the thinking in this case has nothing to do with being right or wrong about something). If the discursive mind is not being stimulated, even though the deeper intuitive faculties are being disposed to the interior quiet that nourishes them, these individuals may soon find themselves hunched over in a snooze. There are worse things that can happen to a person. In this case, some little contemplative aids such as posture and abdominal breathing might help (presuming you are not physically exhausted and in actual need of sleep).

If you sit in a chair, sit up on the edge of it so that you do not use the back of the chair for support. The practice of contemplation is not a leisurely activity. If it were, we would use a hammock or a sofa. Sit up straight, shoulders back, but not rigid, allowing the natural S-curve of the back to support you. Breathe through your nostrils. *Into the Silent Land* shows how proper posture and especially attention to the breath have a long history in the Christian tradition,[7] but the medical world has also been telling us what proper breathing can do.

Breathing deeply through the nasal passages releases nitric oxide, which serves as an effective lung and blood vessel dilator. One effect of this is a sense of being more alert.[8] Ancient wisdom and modern medicine converge on the role of the breath in facilitating alertness during prayer.

Perhaps the most common *versiculum* (prayer word or phrase) is some form of the Jesus Prayer. An aid to praying the Jesus Prayer is such a thing as a Jesus Prayer rope. Like prayer benches, this is quite googleable. Its practical advantage is that it draws in the sense of touch to one's practice. The idea is that the more the body is involved through its posture, breathing, and touching, the more alert we tend to be. Rosaries, common in the Roman Catholic tradition, serve the same purpose, but often there is a lot of discursive meditation that goes along with saying this thoroughly biblical type of prayer. Very often people who have been praying the rosary for a long time are led into the Silence in which Mary conceived the Word made flesh and come to rest in that Silence and only use bits of the prayers associated with the rosary to bring themselves back to that Silence in which the Word is continually born.

These indications will work for some and not for others. Again, remember the words of the Psalmist, "The Lord gives to his beloved while they slumber" (Ps 127:2).

PRAYING WITH ICONS AND STATUES

Icons and statuary make important contributions to any spiritual environment that nurtures prayer. Morning after morning, I used to watch a ninety-eight-year-old woman walk brightly into church and take her usual seat. She would turn her head slightly to the right and give a nod to the statue of Mary and then turn her head a good deal more to the left and wink at the statue of St. Joseph. She would then sit down in her pew and produce a number of prayer cards and place them in a row in front of her. Finally she would reach her arm into her vast purse and pull out yards of rosary. Now ready to begin her prayers, her body assumed an obvious and deep recollection. I don't think she said a word from any of those prayer cards or the rosary. Yet she was convinced she was forgetful during prayer and wanted to hear no talk of what seemed to the naked eye to be the obvious truth: she was immersed in the Silence in which the Word speaks Silence, the depthless depth that all prayer leads to and emerges from.

Statues and icons serve as visual mantras to help us focus.[9] Icons especially seem to open up to us in such a way that we are drawn into them. Some people, in fact, will place an icon in front of them during the time of prayer and use it instead of a prayer word to bring themselves back whenever they become distracted. Not a few people will keep an icon of

Christ or of the Theotokos (Mary with the infant Jesus on her lap) on their desk or some other appropriate place at work. This can be a great help in cultivating a prayerful inner stance throughout the day. But there is a caveat in using external objects: we keep our attention focused on an object of awareness. This has its place in certain formal prayers and communal worship. But those maturing on the path of contemplation will miss the subtler dynamics of contemplation that happen *within awareness* itself and not on the screen of the awareness. At some point, even if it is on our deathbed, a great inner vastness opens up from within awareness. It is not an object of awareness, and it is not our own subjectivity. Embracing both objectivity and subjectivity, it washes onto the shores of perception, an experience people often describe in metaphors of inner spaciousness, abiding calm, luminous vastness. But these labels fail to pin it down, for there is neither the subject nor the object that English syntax demands. Praying with statues and icons has an unquestionably valuable role, but it is a limited role; for it exercises the attention in focusing on external objects of awareness, when the thrust of contemplative practice is to cultivate what is beyond subject-object dualism. One might rightly say that the prayer word is in effect an object of awareness, albeit more interior than an external object like an icon or statue. Indeed it is. That is why we will at some point drop the prayer word; or the prayer word will blossom from within as non-dual awareness—there is simply no one there to pray. There is just an icon, just a statue, just a prayer word, but no separate and independent person who is praying. This is a great inner liberation, the transfer—to use a Pauline metaphor—to the Kingdom of His Beloved Son (see Col 1:12–20). But none of this shows up on a CCTV camera.

I DON'T HAVE TIME TO PRAY

This is something that really separates the sheep from the goats. Tessa Bieleckie once defined the contemplative life as "the art of stealing time." If you have ever spent time in communities of monks or friars or nuns, you will see firsthand that even in communities that officially value contemplation, the practical demands of earning income, keeping rather large premises reasonably clean, and apostolic initiatives leave time for little else other than liturgical prayer (which is certainly better than no prayer at all) and create an in-house culture of going from job to job to job as quickly as possible in order to move on to the next job. On the other hand, I know a woman who has four children under six; she uses their nap time as her prayer time and has mastered the art of praying psalms learnt by heart while doing laundry, preparing meals, housework, breaking up fights, chasing the dog down the street, and doing more laundry. Prayer is not something tacked onto her life but its integrating dynamic.

Some years ago the Jesuit Anthony de Mello was giving a retreat to a community of priests. After he picked up on their resistance to devoting some time each day to quiet prayer, he lambasted them: "Fathers, do not tell me you don't have time to pray. You have time for your cocktails. You have time for your television. Do not tell me you do not have time to pray."

The dynamic of contemplation is easily thwarted if prayer, even regular prayer, is something merely tacked onto our lives, as is the case in most religious communities, whether so-called contemplative or so-called active communities (this dualism is deeply misleading). If we do not allow prayer to assume its natural place as the centering dynamic of life, our prayer life, whether individual or communal, will be like planting seeds in tarmac. We may replant them season after season, but Godot will arrive sooner than any sustained growth and development in prayer. When prayer becomes what orders our day, as something we attempt to live out of moment by moment, rather than the tail pinned blindly onto the donkey of daily life, then prayer will integrate us into itself.

Many dedicated people somehow find a way of reclaiming part of the morning. A steaming mug of coffee or tea creates a lovely liturgical environment of openness and receptivity. The early morning stillness of the house has not been interrupted by telephones, family squabbles, car pools, or doorbells. Some spouses agree to honor this silence between themselves.

Whether we can claim two hours of the morning or twenty minutes or ten minutes, it is important that it be workable on a regular basis. Daily practice is as important as daily nourishment. It does very little good to eat nutritious food once every fortnight and junk food the rest of the time. And so with a contemplative art like sitting in stillness. Carve out of each day something workable, whether it be a portion of the morning, of lunch hour, or of the evening, and go from there.

ON THE ROLE OF THE ENNEAGRAM AND MYERS-BRIGGS IN CONTEMPLATION

In certain circles it is all the rage to figure out how we fare on the enneagram or the Myers-Briggs. On the face of it, these seem to be useful tools for gaining not only a certain amount of self-knowledge, but also a way of understanding how and why we differ from one another. But they run the risk of being reduced to a method of explaining to ourselves why someone else infuriates us: "It's because she is a five on the enneagram," or "He's an INFP on the Myers-Briggs," or an "eight on the Richter Scale!" People find it handy to have clear-cut categories in which to cram the ineffable mystery of the human person. While the enneagram and the Myers-Briggs should not be dismissed as New Age jiggery-pokery, it is disconcerting to see some people's level of identification with these useful instruments of self-knowledge. It should be kept in mind that when we say "I am an eight on the enneagram" or an "INFT on the Myers-Briggs" that we are using the word "am" in an attributive sense, such as "I am blond." Blond is an attribute of a person's hair. I am not blond in the same way that I am Carolyn or Charles. In the latter case, it is an "am" of identity. The enneagram and Myers-Briggs are attributes of our identity. To say "I am an eight and you are a three" is like saying "I am a shirt and you are a jacket."[10] We have a shirt or a jacket that we may really like, but we are not a shirt or a jacket; we can never think they are the seat of identity or that they can definitively pin down personality.

More worryingly, some spiritual directors inform people that according to the results of the Myers-Briggs or the enneagram they should pray in a way that corresponds to that personality type. The person might indeed find this a useful form of prayer, but the dynamics of contemplative simplification happen to all manner of personality types, despite results of personality inventories. If the spiritual director does not recognize the signs that characterize the onset of contemplation (see chapter 5), which can happen to anyone, we end up resisting a process God is initiating. This is another case of what St. John of the Cross calls "hammering the horseshoe instead of the nail," the single action that produces a twofold error: "on the one hand they do harm, and on the other hand they receive no profit."[11]

Yes, there are helpful ways of charting the personality, but there is always something essential about the human person that is unchartable, inscrutable, hidden in mystery. In the Christian view of things, irrespective of whether we put much stock in the enneagram or Myers-Briggs, the essence of human identity is hidden in Mystery, "hidden with Christ in God" (Col 3:3). Irrespective of personality type, the practice of contemplation is concerned with the essence or ground of the person, and this ground is unquantifiable. Helpful as they may be, personality inventories do not go as deep as human beings go.

I SIT THERE AND NOTHING EVER HAPPENS

Some of the most dedicated and prayerful people we will ever meet will claim that their path has been for the most part, if not entirely, dark and dry. Talk of things like "the light of awareness" is not part of the path that they have been traveling for many years, sometimes for decades. Mother Teresa of Calcutta, for example, has shared with us that after very clear early signs of development in her prayer life, she felt darkness and abandonment for most of the time after she founded the Missionaries of Charity.[12] A confrere of mine sat like granite for decades and was a great contemplative support to others, but he himself knew only a dry, dark path; nevertheless he gave himself generously to this path decade after decade. For some people there are explicit encounters of the flowing luminous Vastness, in which we "live and move and have our being" (Acts 17:28). There are yet others who never seem to have any explicit sense of this. Yet I have never met one of these, who walk a dry and dark path, who do not exude calm and virtue of which they were utterly unaware. The real test is prayer's integration into daily life. I can only speak for myself, but I have not met one dedicated person of prayer who walks a very dry, dark path who does not embody many of the cardinal and theological virtues, as well as many of the gifts of the Holy Spirit.[13] By contrast I know many who have had quite explicit contemplative experiences yet have not integrated these experiences into a life of living faith and loving service to their neighbor and even can be mean-spirited and churlish at the slightest provocation.

"We walk by faith and not by sight," (2 Cor 5:7) says St. Paul, who himself struggled for many years to integrate his experience of Light.[14] What is dark to the discursive mind is light to the eyes of faith. The contemplative path is essentially a dry, dark path to the discursive mind. Like a car driving down the road at night, its headlights light up only enough road to see what is just ahead. No more than this. Like the ancient mosaic of Ecclesia, the woman praying with outstretched arms who represents the Church at prayer, we walk with our hands up.

Whether our path be bone dry or bedewed with insight, the health benefits of regular practice are documented increasingly by the medical community. Especially when combined with proper abdominal breathing, there are benefits for hypertension, depression, pain, anxiety, post-traumatic stress disorder, and much more.[15] As the author of *The Cloud of Unknowing* put it centuries before medicine caught on to it, contemplation is good for both body and soul.[16] Even if we sit in silence and "nothing" happens, it would seem that at the very least, health and a sense of well-being happen.

FROM CHARISMATIC PRAYER
TO CONTEMPLATIVE PRAYER

If we have been involved in charismatic prayer for some time, we should not be surprised or disappointed if this style of prayer calms down over the years to a simple resting in the presence of God. The traditional role of God the Holy Spirit is to conform us to God the Word, Who then ushers us into the silent depths of God the Father. This Trinitarian simplification happens at God's own initiative. In early centuries before the Arian controversy that questioned both the divinity of Christ and that of the Holy Spirit, we praised the Trinitarian Mystery not with "Glory be to the Father and to the Son and to the Holy Spirit" but "Glory *to* the Father *through* the Son and *in* the Holy Spirit."[17] The Trinitarian dynamism was more obvious in ancient Christian doxologies. The Holy Spirit's important role is one of simplification, silencing, and conforming us to Jesus the Word Incarnate, Who then leads us into the depths of the Father. This does not happen sequentially but is a threefold dynamism. Whether through the book of nature, the book of Scripture, or the living tradition that binds us all together, the Holy Spirit will one day touch our tongues and bring us to silence before the Unfathomable.

IS IT OKAY TO CHANGE THE PRAYER WORD AND MUST I ALWAYS SAY THE PRAYER WORD?

The default settings, as it were, are to choose a prayer word or phrase and to stick with it, going deeply into the practice via that prayer word or phrase. If you feel drawn simply to sit there, in what St. John of the Cross calls "loving aware-ness," that's okay, too. Stick with that; this is your practice. It is something like planting a seed. We plant the seed, then let it alone so that its energy can go into root and stem growth. If we are frequently replanting the seed, its energy will be put into adjusting to new soil conditions instead of into root and stem production. However, there is no law that says we cannot change our practice if we feel drawn to do so. These are simply values that serve as guidelines.

There is nothing magical or mechanical about the form our practice takes. What we cultivate is interior stillness, and the outer form of our practice facilitates this. Theophan the Recluse reminds us that we should not limit ourselves "to a mechanical repetition of the words of the Jesus Prayer [his prayer phrase]. This will lead to nothing but a habit of repeating the prayer automatically. . . . There is of course nothing wrong with this, but it constitutes only the extreme outer limit of the work."[18] The "power comes from faith in the Lord and from deep union of the mind and heart with Him."[19]

The practice of contemplation involves skills, not techniques. A gardener does not actually grow anything. Plants grow due to their interaction with light, moisture, and nutrients in soil. The gardener cultivates certain skills in order to facilitate a process that the gardener serves. And so with our use of a prayer word or phrase or sitting in loving awareness; it is like gardening: it facilitates a process over which we have no direct control.

What is the equivalent of root and stem production in the seed of our practice? Theophan says your practice "will draw you together."[20] There is an inner process of unification that takes place. The formal aspects of practice (returning to our practice whenever we become aware that we are distracted) change. No longer is our practice something we return to as much as it is something we push off from into something deeper. At a certain point—whether after an hour or half a century—our practice will open up onto depths that are within us and in which we are at the same time immersed. Our practice is like the sides of a pool allowing us to push off into the depths. The formal aspects of practice are only "the instrument and not the essence of the work," and serve these deeper dynamics.[21] What Theophan says of the Jesus Prayer is true of any practice: "Delve deeply into the Jesus Prayer with all the power that you possess."[22]

The prayer word need not always be said any more than a hawk in the sky needs always to flap its wings. As Theophan puts it, "words are only the instrument and not the essence of the work."[23] If we are immersed in our practice, whether or not we are verbally reciting the prayer word is beside the point. It is never a question of fidelity to technique.

CAN THE PRACTICE OF CONTEMPLATION HELP WITH FORGIVENESS?

The practice of contemplation, especially a maturing practice, gives great insight into one of life's great mysteries: the mystery of how to forgive and what forgiveness means and does not mean. Because sitting in stillness on a regular basis gives us plenty of opportunity to look into our thoughts, we soon come to see that we often make a category error when it comes to forgiveness. Many people who think they are struggling to forgive are actually struggling with pain. We keep certain defenses up to protect ourselves from being hurt again, and we interpret this defense as the unwilling-ness or inability to forgive.

We talk to ourselves far too much about an offense that has happened.[24] A cultivated practice of contemplation helps us become aware of this inner chatter and return to our prac-tice or at the very least not attend to this aspect of our minds that talks incessantly about what happened. Sometimes the offending behavior is entirely unremarkable. Sometimes it is incredibly remarkable. In either case, we should be able to distinguish what is pain management and what is a real need to offer or receive forgiveness. Often this takes time.

The old saying "forgive and forget" is unhelpful, even unsafe. What if the offending person is in a drunken state and happens to throw a chair across the kitchen at you. Is it safe or wise to forget that this can happen? There is an implicit understanding that to forgive means that the offending behavior is somehow acceptable. This is not a fair assumption; it is never okay to throw a chair, literally or metaphorically, at someone. Moreover, many of us think we need to wait for the offending person to apologize to us before we can forgive (often by saying "Oh, that's okay"). Sometimes the offender is himself or herself too defended or stupid to realize the damage done.

Saint Diadochos has some helpful advice when it comes to moving into the arena of forgiveness when the other person does not desire reconciliation, or is not even aware of the need for it. He says, "When spiritual knowledge is active within us to a limited degree, it makes us feel acute remorse if, because of sudden irritation, we insult someone and make an enemy of him. It never stops prodding our conscience until, with a full apology, we have restored in the person we have insulted the feelings he had towards us before."[25] The problem with this unresolved state is that it keeps us from moving deeper into prayer, or, as St. Diadochos puts it, it does not "allow the mind to expand."[26] Anger and unresolved conflict can get in the way. Anger leaves aware- ness tight and narrow, whereas the way of compassion and contemplation expands the mind. Saint Diadochos would prod us to pursue forgiveness for our own good as well. But it is not always possible to bring the other person into the circle of forgiveness. They may, for reasons we do not understand, quite simply refuse. Saint Diadochos urges us not to let this get in the way. He offers an exercise where we ourselves can cultivate loving-kindness toward the person, even without the person's cooperation: "If he refuses to lay aside this anger or avoids the places we ourselves frequent, then spiritual knowledge bids us visualize his person with an overflowing of compassion in our soul and so fulfill the law of love in the depths of our heart. For it is said that if we wish to have knowledge of God we must bring our mind to look without anger even on persons who are angry with us for no reason."[27] It is important to remember that "compassion" does not mean sweet sentiment toward a person. Especially if wounds are still fresh, attempts to manufacture positive feelings toward the offender, feelings we do not happen to have, will be counterproductive. Literally "compassion" means to feel with. The word betokens more a felt solidarity with a person than positive feelings for a particular person. We may wish for the well-being of the offender in whom God dwells even while our feelings still hurt. The two are not mutually exclusive. If we lead with compassion, the sentiment and appropriate amount of personal contact will come in due course. As Pauline Matarasso puts it:

> Between us we built a bridge
> Of small fidelities.[28]

Not all relationships get resolved in an ideal manner. This is saddening, to say the least. Saint Diadochos perhaps knows this from his own experience and so extends to us this wisdom for handling a difficulty that besets many relationships.

Notes

INTRODUCTION

1. Isaiah Berlin, *The Hedgehog and the Fox: An Essay on Tolstoy's View of History* (New York: Mentor Books, 1957), 7.

2. St. Teresa of Avila, *The Interior Castle*, 5.4, trans. M. Starr (New York: Riverhead Books, 2004), 145.

3. Ibid. 7.2 (trans. Starr, 270).

4. Ibid.

5. Ibid.

6. See M. Laird, *Into the Silent Land: A Guide to the Christian Practice of Contemplation* (New York: Oxford University Press, 2006).

7. St. Augustine, *Confessions* 3.7, trans. H. Chadwick (Oxford: Oxford University Press, 1991), 43; translation altered.

8. *The Book of Privy Counselling*, chap. 1, in *The Cloud of Unknowing and Other Works*, trans. A. C. Spearing (London: Penguin Books, 2001), 104.

9. Augustine, *Confessions* 5.8 (trans. Chadwick), 100.

10. Ibid., 100.

11. Ibid., 101.

12. Ibid.

13. Gerard Manley Hopkins, "No Worst," in *Selected Poetry*, ed. C. Philips (Oxford: Oxford University Press, 1996), 152.

14. Evagrius, "Outline Teaching on Asceticism and Stillness in the Solitary Life," in *The Phlokalia*, vol. 1, trans. G. Palmer, P. Sherrard, and K. Ware (London: Faber and Faber, 1979), 33.

CHAPTER ONE

1. St. John of the Cross, *The Living Flame of Love* 1.12, in *The Collected Works of St. John of the Cross*, trans. K. Kavanaugh and O. Rodriguez (Washington, D.C.: Institute of Carmelite Studies Publications, rev. ed. 1991), 645.

2. St. Bonaventure, *The Soul's Journey into God* 5.8, in *Bonaventure*, trans. E. Cousins (New York: Paulist Press, 1978), 101. Bonaventure is quoting Alan of Lille, but the saying is pre-Christian, going back at least as far as Hermes Trismegistis, and is cited much later and more famously by Blaise Pascal, *Pensées* 119.

3. Bonaventure, *Soul's Journey into God* 5.8 (trans. E. Cousins, 101).

4. Angelus Silesius, *The Cherubinic Wanderer* 4.156, trans. M. Shrady (New York: Paulist Press, 1986), 96.

5. Ibid. 4.157 (trans. Shrady, 96).

6. St. Augustine, *Confessions* 1.11 (17), trans. H. Chadwick (Oxford: Oxford University Press, 1991), 13.

7. Evagrius, *Talking Back: A Monastic Handbook for Combating Demons, Prologue*, trans. D. Brakke (Collegeville, Minn.: Liturgical Press, 2009), 49.

8. For a rich account of the varied role of Scripture in early Christian monasticism see D. Burton-Christie, *Word in the Desert: Scripture and the Quest for Holiness in Early Christian Monasticism* (New York: Oxford University Press, 1993).

9. See St. Augustine, Letter 130, 20; translation my own.

10. See K. Ware, *The Power of the Name: The Jesus Prayer in Orthodox Spirituality* (Oxford: SLG Press, 1974).

11. St. John Climacus, *The Ladder of Divine Ascent*, chap. 27, trans. C. Luibheid and N. Russell (Mahwah, N.J.: Paulist Press, 1982), 270.

12. Guigo II, *The Ladder of Monks*, trans. E. Colledge, and J. Walshe (Garden City, N.Y.: Image Books, 1978).

13. John of the Cross, *The Sayings of Light and Love* 88, in *Collected Works of St. John of the Cross* (trans. Kavanaugh and Rodriguez, 92).

14. Evagrius, *On Discrimination*, chap. 14, in *The Philokalia*, vol. 1, trans. G. Palmer, P. Sherrard, and K. Ware (London: Faber and Faber, 1979), 47.

15. Simone Weil, "Reflections on the Right Use of School Studies with a View to the Love of God," in *Waiting on God*, trans. E. Crauford (London: Routledge and Kegan Paul, 1979), 51.

16. St. Gregory of Sinai, "The Beginning of Watchfulness," chap. 2, in *Philokalia*, vol. 4, trans. G. Palmer, P. Sherrard, and K. Ware (London: Faber and Faber, 1994), 264. Gregory's further advice to keep the head bent downward should be approached with caution in light of what we know today about the usefulness of straight posture.

17. St. Hesychios, "On Watchfulness and Holiness," chap. 187, in *Philokalia*, vol. 1 (trans. Palmer et al., 195).

18. St. Teresa of Avila, *The Interior Castle* 4.3, trans. M. Starr (New York: Riverhead Books, 2003), 107.

19. Theophan the Recluse, in *The Art of Prayer: An Orthodox Anthology*, comp. Igumen Chariton, trans. E. Kadloubovsky and E. Palmer (London: Faber and Faber, 1966), 90.

20. Meister Eckhart, Sermon 29, in *The Complete Mystical Works of Meister Eckhart*, trans. M. Walshe (New York: Crossroad, 2009), 178.

21. St. Isaac the Syrian, "On Silence," in *The Ascetical Homilies of Isaac the Syrian*, trans. Holy Transfiguration Monastery (Boston: Holy Transfiguration Monastery, 1984), 310; translation altered slightly.

22. *The Cloud of Unknowing*, chap. 7, in *The Cloud of Unknowing and Other Works*, trans. A. C. Spearing (London: Penguin Books, 2001), 29.

CHAPTER TWO

1. The standard biographical source for Evagrius is provided by Palladius, *Lausiac History*, chap. 38, trans. R. Meyer (Westminster, Md.: Newman Press), 110–14; see also the recent English translation of the fuller Coptic version of Palladius's account in *Four Desert Fathers: Pambo, Evagrius, Macarius of Egypt and Macarius of Alexandria*, trans. T. Vivian (Crestwood, N.Y.: St. Vladimir's Seminary Press, 2004), 72–92.

2. Evagrius, *Chapters on Prayer*, chap. 63, in *The Praktikos and Chapters on Prayer*, trans. J. Bamberger (Kalamazoo, Mich.: Cistercian, 1981), 33.

3. Evagrius, *Praktikos*, chap. 46 (trans. Bamberger, 29).

4. Evagrius, *Chapters on Prayer*, chap. 21 (trans. Bamberger, 58).

5. Ibid., chap. 24 (trans. Bamberger, 58).

6. Ibid., chap. 26 (trans. Bamberger, 59).

7. Evagrius, *Praktikos*, chap. 20 (trans. Bamberger, 21).

8. Evagrius, *Chapters on Prayer*, chap. 29 (trans. Bamberger, 59).

9. Jane Austen, *Persuasion* (Oxford: Oxford University Press, 2004), 55.

10. Evagrius, *Praktikos*, chap. 54 (trans. Bamberger, 31).

11. Ibid.

12. Evagrius, *Chapters on Prayer*, chap. 64 (trans. Bamberger, 65; translation adapted).

13. Ibid., chap. 21 (trans. Bamberger, 58; translation altered).

14. Evagrius, *Praktikos*, chap. 7 (trans. Bamberger, 17; translation altered).

15. Ibid., chap. 11 (trans. Bamberger, 18).

16. Ibid., chap. 46 (trans. Bamberger, 21).

17. Ibid., chap. 11 (trans. Bamberger, 18).

18. Ibid., chap. 21 (trans. Bamberger, 21–22).

19. Ibid., chap. 48 (trans. Bamberger, 29).

20. Ibid., chap. 54 (trans. Bamberger, 31).

21. Hesychios, *On Watchfulness and Holiness*, chap. 2, in *The Philokalia*, vol. 1, trans. G. Palmer, P. Sherrard, and K. Ware (London: Faber and Faber, 1979), 162; translation altered.

22. Evagrius, *Praktikos*, chap. 6 (trans. Bamberger, 16–17).

23. Evagrius, *Thoughts*, chaps. 6, 18, and 24 in R. Sinkewicz, trans. *Evagrius Ponticus: The Greek Ascetic Corpus* (Oxford: Oxford University Press, 2003), 157, 165, 170.

24. M. Bullet-Jonas, *Holy Hunger* (New York: Vintage Books, 2000), 64.

25. Hesychius, *On Watchfulness and Holiness*, chap. 70, in *Philokalia*, vol. 1 (trans. Palmer et al., 70; translation altered).

26. By "monk" I intend both male and female monastics; see the provocative essays on this topic by R. Pannikkar and others in *Blessed Simplicity: The Monk as Universal Archetype* (New York: Seabury Press, 1982).

27. St. Theodoros, "A Century of Spiritual Texts," chap. 17, in *The Philokalia*, vol. 2, trans. G. Palmer, P. Sherrard, and K. Ware (London: Faber and Faber, 1981), 17; here I use the translation of J. McGuckin in his *The Book of Mystical Chapters* (Boston: Shambhala, 2002), 57.

28. St. Basil, Letter 2, in *The Letters*, vol. 1, trans. R. Deferrari, Loeb Classical Library (Cambridge, Mass.: Harvard University Press, 1926), 7–9.

29. Horace, Letter 1.11.27, in Q. Horatius Flaccus, *Opera*, 4th ed., ed. D. R. Shackleton Bailey (Leibzig: Teubner, 2001), 272; translation my own.

30. Evagrius, *Praktikos*, chap. 54 (trans. Bamberger, 31).

31. St. Augustine, quoted in *Return to Your Heart*, trans. B. O'Rourke (Clare, Suffolk, England: Augustinian Press, 1995), 44.

32. Evagrius, *Praktikos*, chap. 6 (trans. Bamberger, 17).

33. Ibid.; translation altered slightly.

34. St. Isaac of Nineveh, Homily 3.B34, in *The Wisdom of St. Isaac of Nineveh*, trans. S. Brock (Piscataway, N.J.: Gorgias Press, 2006), 4.

35. D. Scott, "This Meadow, a Soul," *Piecing Together* (Tarset, Northumberland, England: Bloodaxe, 2005), 10.

36. "David Foster Wallace on Life and Work," *Wall Street Journal*, September 19, 2008, http://online.wsj.com/article/SB122178211966454607. html#printMode.

CHAPTER THREE

1. K. Norris, *Amazing Grace: A Vocabulary of Faith* (New York: Riverhead Books, 1998), 28.

2. W. Stevens, "Thirteen Ways of Looking at a Blackbird, V," in *The Collected Poems of Wallace Stevens* (New York: Vintage Books, 1990), 93.

3. R. P. Warren, "The Enclave," in *The Collected Poems of Robert Penn Warren*, ed. J. Burt (Baton Rouge: Louisiana State University Press, 1998), 300–301.

4. See M. Roizen and M. Oz, *You, Staying Young* (New York: Free Press, 2007), 350.

5. Jordan of Saxony, *The Life of the Brethren*, trans. G. Deighan (Villanova, Pa.: Augustinian Press, 1993), 375.

6. See H. Koenig, *Medicine, Religion and Health: Where Science and Religion Meet* (West Conshohocken, Pa.: Templeton Foundation Press, 2008).

7. "The soul's center is God," says St. John of the Cross, *The Living Flame of Love* 1.12, in *The Collected Works of St. John of the Cross* trans. K. Kavanaugh and O. Rodriguez, (Washington, D.C.: Institute of Carmelite Studies, rev. ed. 1991), 645.

8. St. Isaac the Syrian, "On Silence," in *The Ascetical Homilies of Isaac the Syrian*, trans. Holy Transfiguration Monastery (Boston: Holy Transfiguration Monastery, 1984), 310.

9. Ibid.

10. Meister Eckhart, Sermon 1, in *The Complete Mystical Works of Meister Eckhart*, trans. M. Walshe (New York: Crossroad, 2009), 33.

11. Meister Eckhart, *Talks of Instruction* 6, in *Meister Eckhart: Selected Writings*, trans. O. Davies (London: Penguin Books, 1994), 8–9.

12. Ibid., 9.

13. Saint Augustine, *Exposition on Psalm* 139, chap. 15, in *Expositions on the Psalms*, trans. M. Boulding (Hyde Park, N.Y.: New City Press, 2004), 297.

14. "The Quiet Life," trans. C. Thompson, in Thompson, *The Strife of Tongues: Fray Luis de León and the Golden Age of Spain* (Cambridge: Cambridge University Press, 1988), 21.

15. R. S. Thomas, "Adjustments," in *Collected Poems 1945–1990* (London: J. M. Dent, 1993), 345.

CHAPTER FOUR

1. Plotinus, *The Enneads* 1.6.9, trans. Stephen MacKenna (London: Penguin Books, 1991), 54.

2. Amphilochios of Patmos. My thanks to my colleague Dr. Christopher Haas for directing me to this author.

3. St. Teresa of Avila, *The Interior Castle* 1.2, trans. M. Starr (New York: Riverhead Books, 2004), 45.

4. St. Augustine, Sermon 88.5, in *The Works of St. Augustine*, pt. 3, bk. 3, trans. E. Hill (Brooklyn, N.Y.: New City Press, 1991), 422.

5. Teresa of Avila, *Interior Castle* 1.2 (trans. Starr, 45).

6. Ibid. 7.1 (trans. Starr, 262).

7. St. Augustine, *Confessions* 10.2.2, trans. H. Chadwick (Oxford: Oxford University Press, 1998), 179.

8. S. Heaney, "Sunlight," in *North* (London: Faber and Faber, 1975), 8.

9. St. John of the Cross, *The Sayings of Light and Love* 88, in *The Collected Works of St. John of the Cross*, trans. K. Kavanaugh and O. Rodriguez, (Washington, D.C.: Institute of Carmelite Studies, rev. ed. 1991), 92.

10. St. Hesychios, *On Watchfulness and Holiness*, chap. 1, in *The Philokalia*, vol. 1, trans. G. Palmer, P. Sherrard, and K. Ware (London: Faber and Faber, 1979), 162; translation altered slightly. Hesychios uses the Greek word *nēpsis,* which I translate here as "awareness" to serve as an umbrella term to cover different aspects of awareness such as alertness, sobriety, watchfulness, attentiveness, mindfulness.

11. Ibid.

12. Ibid.

13. Ibid.

14. Hesychios, *On Watchfulness and Holiness*, chap. 166, in *Philokalia*, vol. 1 (trans. Palmer et al., 191; translation altered slightly).

15. See D. Cornell, *A Priceless View* (Maryknoll, N.Y.: Orbis, 2003), 23 and 113.

16. Teresa of Avila, *Interior Castle* 7.2 (trans. Starr, 270).

17. Ibid. 1.2 (trans. Starr, 42).

18. Ibid. (trans. Starr, 49).

19. St. Diadochos, *On Spiritual Knowledge*, chap. 26, in *Philokalia*, vol. 1 (trans. Palmer et al., 259).

20. Hesychios, *On Watchfulness and Holiness*, chap. 103, in *Philokalia*, vol. 1 (trans. Palmer et al., 180).

21. Ibid., chap. 90, in *The Philokalia*, vol. 1 (trans. Palmer et al., 177).

22. Teresa of Avila, *Interior Castle* 4.1 (trans. M. Starr, 91–92).

23. Hesychios, *On Watchfulness and Holiness*, chap. 2, in *Philokalia,* vol. 1 (trans. Palmer et al., 162; translation adapted).

24. Ibid., chap. 14, in *The Philokalia*, vol. 1 (trans. Palmer et al., 164).

25. Evagrius, *Talking Back: A Monastic Handbook for Combating Demons*, trans. D. Brakke (Collegeville, Minn.: Liturgical Press, 2010), prologue, 49.

26. Evagrius, *Praktikos*, chap. 43 (trans. J. Bamberger, 28; translation altered slightly).

27. Ibid., chap. 50 (trans. J. Bamberger, 30).

28. Ibid.

29. Hesychios, *On Watchfulness and Holiness,* chap. 15, in *Philokalia*, vol. 1 (trans. Palmer et al., 164).

30. Ibid., chap. 15, in *Philokalia*, vol. 1(trans. Palmer et al., 164).

31. Ibid., chap. 130, in *Philokalia*, vol. 1 (trans. Palmer et al., 185).

32. Ibid.; translation adapted.

33. Diadochos, *On Spiritual Knowledge*, chap. 26, in *Philokalia*, vol. 1 (trans. Palmer et al., 259).

34. Hesychios, *On Watchfulness and Holiness*, chap. 166, in *Philokalia*, vol. 1 (trans. Palmer et al., 191).

35. Ibid.

36. See the entry "heart" in the glossary of *Philokalia*, vol. 1 (trans. Palmer et al., 361).

37. D. Scott, "This Meadow, a Soul," in *Piecing Together* (Tarset, Northumberland, England: Bloodaxe, 2005), 10.

38. Evagrius, *Chapters on Prayer*, chap. 61, in *The Praktikos and Chapters on Prayer*, trans. J. Bamberger (Kalamazoo, Mich.: Cistercian, 1981), 65; translation altered slightly.

39. Hesychios, *On Watchfulness and Holiness*, chap. 7, in *Philokalia*, vol. 1(trans. Palmer et al., 163; translation altered slightly).

40. St. Augustine, *Exposition of Psalm 62*, 15, trans. M. Boulding, in *Expositions of the Psalms*, vol. 3 (Hyde Park, N.Y.: New City Press, 2001), 241–42.

41. St. Maximus the Confessor, *Quaestionis ad Thalassium* 64, in *Patrologia Graeca* 90.760A, my translation. See also Augustine, *Confessions* 1.4 (trans. Chadwick, 5).

42. St. Isaac the Syrian, "On Silence," in *The Ascetical Homilies of Isaac the Syrian*, trans. Holy Transfiguration Monastery (Boston: Holy Transfiguration Monastery, 1984), 310.

43. Hesychios, *On Watchfulness and Holiness*, chap. 50, in *Philokalia*, vol. 1 (trans. Palmer et al., 171).

44. Ibid., chap. 90, in *Philokalia*, vol. 1(trans. Palmer et al., 177).

45. Ibid., chap. 166, in *Philokalia*, vol. 1(trans. Palmer et al., 191).

46. Teresa of Avila, *Interior Castle* 7.1 (trans. Starr, 261).

47. Hesychios, *On Watchfulness and Holiness*, chap. 103, in *Philokalia*, vol. 1 (trans. Palmer et al., 180).

48. Ibid., chap. 90, in *Philokalia*, vol. 1(trans. Palmer et al., 180).

49. Augustine, *Confessions* 7.7, trans. Pine-Coffin (London: Penguin Books, 1961), 143; translation altered slightly.

50. Diadochos, *On Spiritual Knowledge*, chap. 49, in *Philokalia*, vol. 1 (trans. Palmer et al., 265).

51. Augustine, *Confessions* 10.27; my translation.

52. Heaney, "Sunlight."

53. Augustine, *Confessions* 3.4 (trans. Chadwick, 43).

54. Compare St. Bonaventure, *The Soul's Journey into God* 5.8, in *Bonaventure*, trans. E. Cousins (New York: Paulist Press, 1978), 101.

55. See Augustine, Sermon 88.5 (trans. Hill), 422.

56. See Augustine, *Confessions* 8.8 (trans. Chadwick, 120–21).

57. R. S. Thomas, "Mass for Hard Times," in *Collected Later Poems 1988–2000* (Tarset, Northumberland, England: Bloodaxe Books, 2004), 136.

58. Augustine, *Confessions* 7.7 (trans. Pine-Coffin, 143; translation altered slightly).

59. Evagrius, *Chapters on Prayer,* chap. 74, in *Philokalia*, vol. 1 (trans. Palmer et al., 64).

60. Diadochos, *On Spiritual Knowledge*, chap. 40, in *Philokalia*, vol. 1 (trans. Palmer et al., 265).

61. Ibid.

62. Teresa of Avila, *Interior Castle* 5.4 (trans. Starr, 145).

63. St. John of the Cross, *The Living Flame of Love* 2.10, in *Collected Works of St. John of the Cross* (trans. Kavanaugh and Rodriguez, 661).

64. Augustine, *Confessions* 10.34 (trans. Chadwick, 209).

CHAPTER FIVE

1. R. S. Thomas, "AD," in *Collected Later Poems 1988–2000* (Tarset, Northumberland, England: Bloodaxe Books, 2004), 118.

2. St. Augustine, *Confessions* 4.12, trans. H. Chadwick (Oxford: Oxford University Press), 64.

3. St. Augustine, cited in *Return to Your Heart*, trans. B. O'Rourke (Clare, Suffolk, England: Augustinian Press, 2002), 6.

4. *The Book of Privy Counselling*, chap. 2, in *The Cloud of Unknowing and Other Works*, trans. A. C. Spearing (London: Penguin Books, 2001), 106; translation altered slightly; emphasis added.

5. *The Ascent of Mount Carmel* 2.13.1–9, in *The Collected Works of St. John of the Cross*, trans. K. Kavanaugh and O. Rodriguez, (Washington, D.C.: Institute of Carmelite Studies, rev, ed., 1991), 89.

6. *The Living Flame of Love* 3.32, in *Collected Works of St. John of the Cross* (trans. Kavanaugh and Rodriguez, 685).

7. *Ascent* 2.13.3 (trans. Kavanaugh and Rodriguez, 189).

8. Ibid. 2.13.4 (trans. Kavanaugh and Rodriguez, 189–90).

9. St. Athanasius, *The Life of St. Anthony,* in *Athanasius: The Life of St. Anthony and the Letter to Marcellinus,* trans. R. Gregg (New York: Paulist Press, 1980), 31.

10. Dietrich Bonhoeffer, *Life Together,* trans. D. Bloesch, J. Burtness, ed. G. Kelley, in *Dietrich Bonhoeffer Works,* vol. 5 (Minneapolis: Fortress Press, 1996), 83.

11. *The Dark Night* 10.4, in *Collected Works of St. John of the Crosss* (trans. Kavanaugh and Rodriguez, 382).

12. Ibid., translation altered slightly.

13. *Living Flame of Love* 3.45 (trans. Kavanaugh and Rodriguez, 691).

14. Ibid., translation adapted.

15. He is paraphrasing St. John Climacus, *The Ladder of Perfection,* chap. 27, trans. C. Luibheid and N. Russell (New York: Paulist Press, 1982), 270.

16. *Dark Night* 10.5 (trans. Kavanaugh and Rodriguez, 382).

17. Ibid.

18. Ibid. 1.10.5 (trans. Kavanaugh and Rodriguez, 382; translation altered).

19. Ibid. 1.10.4 (trans. Kavanaugh and Rodriguez, 382; translation altered).

20. *Sayings of Light and Love* 88 (trans. Kavanaugh and Rodriguez, 92).

21. Ibid. 119 (trans. Kavanaugh and Rodriguez, 94).

22. Ibid. 132 (trans. Kavanaugh and Rodriguez, 95; translation altered). The same teaching is found in the postscript to Letter 8 (trans. Kavanaugh and Rodriguez, 742).

23. S. T. Coleridge, *Rime of the Ancient Mariner,* lines 244–47, in *Poetical Works,* ed. E. Coleridge (1912; reprint, Oxford: Oxford University Press, 1986), 197.

24. Evagrius, *The Praktikos,* chap. 49, in *The Praktikos and Chapters on Prayer,* trans. J. Bamberger (Kalamazoo, Mich.: Cistercian, 1981), 29; translation altered slightly.

25. For "mind" he uses the Greek word *nous,* sometimes translated as "spirit," instead of a word such as *dianoia,* which would indicate the thinking mind.

26. This is well described by K. Ware, "Prayer in Evagrius of Pontus and the Macarian Homilies," in R. Waller and B. Ward, eds., *An Introduction to Christian Spirituality* (London: SPCK, 1999), 14–19.

27. *Sayings of Light and Love*, 117 (trans. Kavanaugh and Rodriguez, 93; translation altered slightly).

28. Coleridge, *Rime of the Ancient Mariner*, lines 117–118, in *Poetical Works*, 191.

29. J. Chapman, *Spiritual Letters* (London: Sheed and Ward, 1935), 179.

30. Ibid., 108.

31. St. Teresa of Avila, *The Way of Perfection*, chap. 30, in *The Collected Works of St. Teresa of Avila*, vol. 2, trans. K. Kavanaugh and O. Rodriguez (Washington, D.C.: Institute of Carmelite Studies, 1980), 152.

32. John Keats, "Ode on a Grecian Urn," in *The Complete Poetry and Selected Prose of John Keats*, ed. Harold Edgar Briggs (New York: Modern Library, 1951), 295.

CHAPTER SIX

1. Mark Twain, *The Adventures of Huckleberry Finn* (London: Penguin Books, 2003), 51.

2. There is a growing body of literature documenting the usefulness of the practice of contemplation in the treatment of depression. See for example, Z. Segal, J. Williams, and J. Teasdale, eds., *Mindfulness-Based Cognitive Therapy for Depression* (New York: Guilford Press, 2002).

3. There are many forms of depression with differing psychogeneses. Josh's is just one form, but practice of contemplation and awareness is acknowledged by many cognitive behavioral psychologists to be an effective component of recovery and maintenance; see note 2.

4. See Elizabeth of the Trinity, *The Complete Works,* vol.1 (Washington, D.C.: Institute of Carmelite Studies, 1984), 179.

5. St. Diadochos, *On Spiritual Knowledge*, chap. 26, in *The Philokalia*, vol. 1, trans. G. Palmer, P. Sherrard, and K. Ware (London: Faber and Faber, 1979), 259.

6. St. Hesychios, *On Watchfulness and Holiness*, chap. 27, in *Philokalia*, vol. 1 (trans. Palmer et al., 166; translation abbreviated slightly).

7. See Leo Tolstoy, *The Death of Ivan Ilyich*, trans. L. Solotarov (New York: Bantam Books, 1981), 134.

8. *The Cloud of Unknowing*, chap. 32, in *The Cloud of Unknowing and Other Works*, trans. A. C. Spearing (London: Penguin Books, 2001), 55.

9. Hesychios, *On Watchfulness and Holiness*, chap. 166, in *Philokalia*, vol. 1 (trans. Palmer et al., 191).

10. *Cloud of Unknowing*, chap. 32 (trans. Spearing, 55).

11. Meister Eckhart, Sermon 25, in *Meister Eckhart: Selected Writings*, trans. O. Davies (London: Penguin Books, 1994), 228.

12. Heyschios, *On Watchfulness and Holiness*, chap. 166, in *Philokalia* vol. 1 (trans. Palmer et al., 191).

13. Ibid.

14. St. John of the Cross, Letter 20, in *The Collected Works of St. John of the Cross*, trans. K. Kavanaugh and O. Rodriguez, (Washington, D.C.: Institute of Carmelite Studies, rev. ed., 1991), 755–56.

15. The letter is addressed to an unnamed Carmelite nun.

16. Ibid., 755.

17. Ibid., 755.

18. Ibid., 756.

19. New Testament scholars remind us that there is no necessary connection between Mary Magdalene and the unnamed woman caught in adultery (Jn 8:3–4) or the unnamed woman of ill repute (Lk 7:37); for exegetical purposes patristic and mediaeval theologians tended to collapse all these figures into the one figure, Mary Magdalene.

20. *Cloud of Unknowing*, chap. 16 (trans. Spearing, 41).

21. Pauline Matarasso, "And Therefore She Hung Up Her Love and Her Longing Desire in This Cloud of Unknowing," in *The Price of Admission* (Cambridge, England: Broughton House Books, 2005), 74.

22. St. John of the Cross, *The Sayings of Light and Love* 132, in *Collected Works of St. John of the Cross* (trans. Kavanaugh and Rodriguez, 95; translation altered slightly).

23. St. Teresa of Avila, *The Interior Castle* 7.2, trans. M. Starr (New York: Riverhead Books, 2003), 274.

CHAPTER SEVEN

1. St. John of the Cross, *The Dark Night* 2.10.3, in *The Collected Works of St. John of the Cross*, trans. K. Kavanaugh and O. Rodriguez (Washington, D.C.: Institute of Carmelite Studies, rev. ed., 1991), 417.

2. F. O'Connor, "Greenleaf," in *The Complete Stories* (New York: Noonday, 1995), 333.

3. St. John of the Cross, *Dark Night* 2.10.1 (trans. Kavanaugh and Rodriguez, 46).

4. Ibid.

5. St. John of the Cross, *The Living Flame of Love* 1.20, in *Collected Works of St. John of the Cross* (trans. Kavanaugh and Rodriguez, 648–49).

6. St. Grégoire de Nysse, *De Vita Moysis* 2.165, ed. and French trans. J. Daniélou, in *Sources Chrétiennes,* vol. 1bis (Paris: Les Éditions du Cerf, 1987), 212; my translation.

7. St. Thomas Aquinas, *Super De Trinitate*, pars 1 q. 1 a 2 ad 1, Latin text from the on-line *Index Thomisticus*; my translation.

8. St. Gregory of Nyssa, *The Beatitudes* 6, in St. Gregory of Nyssa, *The Lord's Prayer and The Beatitudes*, trans. H. Graef (New York: Newman Press, 1954), 143.

9. St. Grégoire de Nysse, *Homélies sur L'Ecclésiaste* 7.8, ed. P. Alexander and French trans. F. Vinel, in *Sources Chrétiennes,* vol. 416 (Paris: Les Éditions du Cerf, 1996) 382; my translation.

10. St. John of the Cross, *Dark Night* 2.10.1 (trans. Kavanaugh and Rodriguez, 416).

11. Ibid.

12. Ibid.

13. M. C. Richards, *Centering in Pottery, Poetry and the Person*, 2nd ed. (Middletown, Conn.: Wesleyan University Press, 1989), 133.

14. St. John of the Cross, *Dark Night* 2.10.3 (trans. Kavanaugh and Rodriguez, 417).

CHAPTER EIGHT

1. Mark Twain, *The Adventures of Huckleberry Finn* (London: Penguin Books, 1985), 19.
2. Ibid., 19.
3. Ibid., 48.
4. Pseudo-Dionysius the Areopagite, *The Divine Names* 3.1 in *Pseudo-Dionysius: The Complete Works*, trans. C. Luibheid (New York: Paulist Press, 1987), 68; translation altered slightly. Despite the fact that we now know this author was not the Athenian convert of Paul, there is a current convention to drop the prefix "pseudo" due to his great influence on both the Christian East and West and refer to him in the Christian West simply as Dionysius or Denys the Areopagite.
5. Ibid. 3.1 (trans. Luibheid), 69.
6. Ibid. 2.5 (trans. Luibheid), 62.
7. M. Laird, *Into the Silent Land* (New York: Oxford University Press, 2006), 36–45; for a fuller development see M. Laird, "Continually Breathe Jesus Christ: Stillness and Watchfulness in *The Philokalia*," *Communio* 34 (2007), 243–63.
8. M. Roizen and M. Oz, *You: Staying Young* (New York: Free Press, 2007), 132.
9. I owe this term "visual mantra" to a very helpful person I met at a workshop in San Diego in October 2009.
10. I draw this metaphor from an audio recording of Antoinette Varner (Gangagi).
11. St. John of the Cross, *The Living Flame of Love* 3.45, in *The Collected Works of St. John of the Cross*, trans. K. Kavanaugh and O. Rodriguez, (Washington, D.C.: Institute of Carmelite Studies, rev. ed. 1991), 691.
12. See *Come Be My Light*, ed. B. Kolodiejchuk (New York: Doubleday, 2007).
13. The cardinal virtues: prudence, justice, fortitude, temperance; the theological virtues: faith, hope, and love; the gifts of the Holy Spirit: wisdom, understanding, counsel, courage, knowledge, piety, fear of the Lord.

14. See J. Ashton, *The Religion of Paul the Apostle* (New Haven: Yale University Press, 2000).

15. See H. Koenig, *Medicine, Religion, and Health: Where Science and Spirituality Meet* (Conshohocken, Pa.: Templeton Foundation Press, 2008); see also E. D'Aquilli and A. Newberg, *The Mystical Mind: Probing the Biology of Religious Experience* (Minneapolis: Fortress Press, 1999).

16. *The Cloud of Unknowing*, chap. 54, in *The Cloud of Unknowing and Other Works*, trans A. C. Spearing (London: Penguin Books, 2001), 78.

17. Sara Grant, *Towards an Alternative Theology* (Notre Dame, Ind.: University of Notre Dame Press, 2002), 12.

18. *The Art of Prayer: An Orthodox Anthology*, comp. Igumen Chariton (London: Faber and Faber, 1966), 99–100.

19. Ibid., 99.

20. Ibid., 90–91.

21. Ibid.

22. Ibid.

23. Ibid.

24. See F. Luskin, *Forgive for Good* (San Francisco: HarperSanFranciso, 2002).

25. St. Diadochos, *On Spiritual Knowledge*, chap. 92, in *The Philokalia*, vol 1., trans. G. Palmer, P. Sherrard, and K. Ware (London: Faber and Faber, 1979), 290.

26. Ibid.

27. Ibid.

28. P. Matarasso, "Betrayal," in *The Price of Admission* (Cambridge, England: Broughton House Books, 2005), 40.